THE BOOK OF JASHER

THE BOOK OF JASHER

WITH

TESTIMONIES AND NOTES,

CRITICAL AND HISTORICAL, EXPLANATORY OF THE TEXT.

TO WHICH IS PREFIXED,

VARIOUS READINGS,

AND

A PRELIMINARY DISSERTATION,

PROVING THE AUTHENTICITY OF THE WORK.

Translated into English from the Hebrew,

BY

FLACCUS ALBINUS ALCUINUS, OF BRITAIN.

KALPAZ

ISBN: 978-93-5128-991-3(HB)

First Published in 1829
Indian Reprint in 2017

Published by

Kalpaz Publications
C-30, Satyawati Nagar,
Delhi – 110052
E-mail: kalpaz@hotmail.com
Website: kalpazpublications.com
Ph.: +91-9212142040

Cataloging in Publication Data—DK
Courtesy: D.K. Agencies (P) Ltd. <docinfo@dkagencies.com>

Sefer ha-yashar (Quasi-historical work). English.
The Book of Jasher : with testimonies and notes, critical and historical, explanatory of the text, to which is prefixed, various readings, and a preliminary dissertation, proving the authenticity of the work / translated into English from the Hebrew by Flaccus Albinus Alcuinus, of Britain.
pages cm
"First published in 1829"
ISBN 9789351289913 (HB)

1. Bible. Hexateuch—Paraphrases, English—Early works to 1800. 2. Aggada—Early works to 1800. I. Ilive, Jacob, 1705-1763. II. Alcuin, 735-804, translator. III. Title.

BS1216.S44 2017 DDC 296.19 23

ADVERTISEMENT.

THE following translation of "The Book of Jasher," was discovered by a gentleman in a journey through the North of England, in 1721. It lay by him for several years, until, in 1750, there was a rumour of a new translation of the Bible, when he laid it before a noble Earl. On perusal, he highly approved of it, as a work of great sincerity, plainness, and truth. His lordship's opinion was, that it should have been placed in the Bible, before the Book of Joshua.

He further adds, "By a writing on the outside of the manuscript, it should seem that this translation was laid before our first reformers, because it says: 'I have read the Book of Jasher twice over; and I much approve of it, as a piece of great antiquity and curiosity; but I cannot assert, that it should be made a part of the Canon of Scripture. Signed, WICKLIFFE.'"

Since 1751, the manuscript has been preserved with great care, by a gentleman who lived to a very advanced age, and died some time since. On the event of his death, a friend to whom he had presented it, gave it to the present Editor, who, conceiving that so valuable a piece of antiquity should not be lost to men of literature, and biblical students, has committed it to the press, not doubting but that the attention of the learned will be attracted to so singular a volume.

The Editor cannot assert any thing from his own knowledge, beyond Alcuin's account, but *that* carries with it such an air of probability and truth, that he does not doubt its authenticity. Some account of this volume may be found in Alcuin's works, published in one volume, fol. in the year 1600, in Paris. He died in 804. Should any gentleman possess a transcript, or copy of it, the Editor will be greatly obliged by any communication made to him, through the medium of the Printer.

PRELIMINARY DISSERTATION

ON THE

ANTIQUITY AND AUTHENTICITY

OF

THE BOOK OF JASHER.

WHEN a work of this nature is brought before the public, it is highly expedient to adduce evidence of its authenticity, which must resolve itself into the external and historical, and then, the internal proofs of its originality.

As to the former of these, it is evident, that such a book existed in the days of Joshua, and that it also continued to be referred to in the time of the Royal Psalmist, David. It appears to have been preserved by the Judges, first, and afterward, by the kings of Judah, until the period of the Babylonish Captivity; after which event, it is not referred to, either by the Prophets, or by the Chronologists of the Jewish nation; a full proof that it was not brought back to Judea. It must then, of course, have been possessed by the kings of Persia, in which country it was found by Alcuin, who was the honour of our own country, and the great ornament of the Court of Charlemagne. This great prince, it appears, engaged his attendance on his person, and received instruction in the sciences from him. He also was present with him at the Council of Frankfort; and, as a reward of his distinguished merit, endowed him with three rich abbies. When he left his court and returned to England, he was further promoted to be Abbot of Canterbury. Alcuin founded the University of Paris, in 800.

The account of his pilgrimage to the Holy Land, and to Persia, is given by himself. His object in remaining at Gazna, for three years, was his obtaining this single piece of antiquity, which cost him in wedges of gold, at least £500, which, at this distance of time, would have amounted to four times that sum. He describes the roll on which it was written in large Hebrew characters of the earliest form, as being two feet nine inches wide, and nine feet in length, and, according to his relation, preserved in the original ark of gopher wood, adorned with Mosaic work, though in a state of decay, from the injuries of time.

Nothing can be produced to invalidate this authentic statement, and, consequently, it merits our credence. It could not be brought forward by him, to answer any end of a secular nature, as it appears he never made it public, beyond the circle of his friends, and when grown old, he left it, with his other manuscripts, to a friend, a priest in Yorkshire. Its preservation from one hand to another, for so many centuries, is easily accounted for, both from its intrinsic merit, and its extraordinary character.

Its having been known to our first reformers, is evident from the testimony of that illustrious leader, Wickliffe. Its falling afterward into neglect, might have been caused from the very few learned men who lived in the following dark ages of Popish ignorance; when little was known, even by the priesthood, beyond their missals, litanies, and breviaries.

The manner of its being brought to light, about a century since, was quite accidental; but then being laid before a distinguished nobleman, who appears to have been high in office, on the most important occasion, that of a new translation of the sacred Scriptures, when he delivered his judgment of it, as a work of great sincerity, plainness, and truth, and whose opinion of it was, that the book of Jasher ought to have been printed in the Bible before the book of Joshua.

From that time, it appears to have been preserved only for its antiquity and curiosity, till it fell into the present Editor's possession, who, on perusing it, saw sufficient reason for its publication, especially as it supplies a chasm in the history of the Judges, from the death of Joshua, including the elders who outlived him, and judged Israel. These are Caleb, who judged Israel twelve years; Jasher, who succeeded him, and Othniel, who saved Israel from Chushan Rishathaim; and then the events are recorded in regular succession of the succeeding Judges.

One of the most remarkable circumstances is, that this book is not more frequently referred to, but that I account for on this principle, that it was not regarded as an inspired work, as the books of Moses were. It makes no claim of that nature, Jasher declaring that he received his information from Caleb, his father, and Hezron, his grandfather, and from Azuba, his mother. This applies to the events which occurred before his own times. He afterwards records facts, as they arose, and states them with the simplicity and force of truth. They agree, in general, with the statements in the books of Moses, and where they differ, it appears that he relates one series of facts, which are not narrated by Moses, although likely to have occurred at the same time. But it is remarkable, that Jasher does not ascribe the causes which gave birth to the events narrated by him, nor does he introduce his commands with the authority of a lawgiver, or proclaim them, as Moses did, with "Thus saith the Lord."

As a book of record, it appears to have truth without mixture of error, for its peculiar object and design. His name, Jasher, or the Upright, seems to stamp all his words and actions, and his counsels and laws are dictated by love to his countrymen, zeal for the honour of God, and a regard to the welfare of his people and nation, and their posterity, for whom he prays with ardour and affection to the time of his death.

I come now to the internal evidence, which verifies the authenticity of this work, and proves it the very genuine production of JASHER. He begins with the creation of the world, and, in a manner similar to Moses, relates the first production of this system. There is a perfect accordance in his account of the formation of light, which he says, shone forth from the firmament and enlightened the abyss; and the abyss fled before the face of the light, and divided between the light and the darkness; so that the face of nature was formed a second time. Then he proceeds to relate the formation of the sun and moon, which he says appeared in the firmament, the one to rule the light, and the other to rule the darkness. His account of the creation of man is truly sublime, and determines a point of the highest importance, the immortality of the soul. The question has long been agitated as to the sense in which the image of God, in which man was made, consisted. Here is a testimony of infinite value in the solution of this point, and worthy of being recorded in every language under the face of the heavens. It answers all the learned arguments of Doctor Warburton, in his divine legation of Moses, proving the great doctrine of the immortality of the soul, and a future state of rewards and punishments, to have been the undoubted judgment of the first patriarchs. The grandeur of this passage exceeds all the strains of human description. "And when all these things were fulfilled, behold JEHOVAH appeared in Eden, and created man, and made him to be an image of his own eternity." This passage proves that the first ages were fully convinced that man is formed for eternity, capable of immortality, and ordained for a never-ending existence, and, consequently, an heir of everlasting happiness or misery.

This doctrine established, all the offices of religion, morality, and humanity flow from it. Man must be an accountable being, and ordained by his glorious Creator to live for ever.

It is to be observed, that the fall of man, the promise of the woman's seed, and the early predictions of a deliverer, are not mentioned by Jasher; nor does he at all allude to any of the predictions in the books of Moses, excepting those of his song, in which the future fates of the tribes are predicted. Shall we determine this to have arisen from his knowledge, that these subjects were designed to be revealed by the Hebrew lawgiver, or from his ignorance of them? It appears to me, that his book is simply a work of record, and not of revelation or prediction, and that the divine mysteries were appointed to be made known by one greater than JASHER, his master and teacher.

The words of Alcuin, which are to be read before *The Book of Jasher.*

I,* Alcuin, of Britain, was minded to travel into the Holy Land, and into the province of Persia, in search of holy things, and to see the wonders of the east. And I took unto me two companions, who learned with me, under able teachers and masters, all those languages which the pèople of the east speak; namely, Thomas of Malmsbury, and John of Huntingdon: and though we went as pilgrims, yet we took with us, silver, and gold, and riches. And when we came unto Bristol, we went into a ship bound for Rome, where we tarried six months, and learned more perfectly the old Persic language. Here the Pope blessed us, and said, Be of resolution, for the work ye have undertaken is of the Lord. From Rome we went to Naples, and tarried there three days, and from thence to Salermo, and from thence to Palermo. We went through Sicily, and took Melita in our way, where we abode six days. Hence we sailed for the Morea, visited Athens, Thessalonia, Constantinople, Philadelphia, Pergamus, Smyrna, Ephesus, Antioch, Coloss, Cappadocia, Alexandria, Damascus, Samaria, Bethel, and Jerusalem. Here we stayed six weeks, and the patriarch John received us kindly. And after having visited every part of the Holy Land, particularly Bethlehem, Hebron, Mount Sinai, and the like, we crossed an arm of the Persic Gulph at Bassora, and went in a boat to Bagdad, and from thence by land to Ardevil, and so to Casbin. Here we learnt from an Ascetic, that at the furthermost part of Persia, in the city of Gazna, was a manuscript, wrote in Hebrew, of *The Book of Jasher.* He stimulated us to this undertaking, by observing, that *The Book of Jasher* was twice mentioned in the *Holy Bible,* and twice appealed to as a book of Testimony, and that it was extant before the writings which are now stiled, *The Books of Moses.* We immediately undertook the journey, going by the way of Ispahan, where we tarried three weeks; at length we arrived at Gazna. Here we laid aside the pilgrims' dress, and I hired a house, where we dwelt during our stay in this city, which was about three years.

I soon became acquainted with the keeper of the library which belongs to the community of this city, and enquired of him concerning *The Book of Jasher,* which the recluse at Casbin had told us of. He said, he had read of such a manuscript in the catalogue of the library, but had never seen it, though he had been custos for

* Alcuin lived in the eighth century. See Biography of Alcuinus Flaccus.

forty-five years, but that it was locked up in a chest, and kept among the pieces of antiquities in a separate part of the library. As I lived nigh the custos, so I soon became familiar in his family; wherefore one day I took the opportunity to tell the custos, that I was very much obliged to him for the civilities he had shewn me, and particularly for the free access he had given me to the library; at the same time I made him a present of a wedge of gold, in value fifty pounds, which he readily accepted. The next time I went to the library, I begged the favour I might see *The Book of Jasher*. He then immediately turned to the catalogue, where it was written, *The Volume of Jasher*. He conducted me into a long room, where he shewed me the chest it was in. He now informed me, that the key was in the hands of the city-treasurer, and that, upon proper application, I might see the volume. The custos introduced me to the treasurer, and related to him the substance of my request. He smiled, and said, he was not then at leisure, but he would consider of it. The next morning I sent John of Huntingdon to the treasurer with a wedge of gold of the value of one hundred pounds, by way of a present. By John, he sent me word, that he would meet me at the library about the ninth hour.

The time being come, the treasurer, the custos, and I, met at the library, when the treasurer having unlocked the chest, shewed me the book, which he called, *The Volume of Jasher*. And then he locked the chest, and gave the key to the custos, telling him, that it was permitted that I might read in the volume, as often as I would, in the presence of the custos, and in the library.

The Book of Jasher is a great scroll, in width, two feet three inches, and in length about nine feet. It is written in large characters, and exceeding beautiful. The paper on which it is written is for thickness the eighth of an inch. To the touch it seemed as soft as velvet, and to the eye as white as snow.

The ark is of Mosaic work, finely and curiously wrought, but time and accidents have very much defaced the external ornaments of it.

After this I had free access to *The Book of Jasher*. The first thing which commanded my attention was a little scroll, intitled, *The story of the Volume of Jasher*. This informed me, that Jasher was born in Goshen, in the land of Egypt, that he was the son of the mighty Caleb, who was general of the Hebrews, whilst Moses was with Jethro in Midian; that on the embassy to Pharaoh, Jasher was appointed virger to Moses and Aaron, to bear the rod before them; that as he always accompanied Moses, Jasher must have the greatest opportunities, of knowing the facts he hath recorded; that from his great attachment to truth and uprightness, he early received his name, ישר; that it was a common saying in Israel of him, *Behold the upright man;* that Jasher wrote the volume which bears his name; that the ark was made in his life-time; that he put the volume therein with his own hands; that Jazer, the eldest son of Jasher, kept it during his life; that the princes of Judah successively were custoes thereof; that the ark and book in the last Babylonish Captivity was taken from the Jews, and so fell into the hands of the Persian monarchs; and that the city of Gazna had been the place of its residence for some hundred years.

This excited in me a great desire of reading the volume itself. The work was divided into thirty-seven parts or portions. One of these portions I read at this time, and so two every day until I had read the whole through. The custos then informed me, that there were in the two side boxes of the chest, certain notes or remarks, which some of the ancients had made on several passages contained in *The Book of Jasher*. These also I read.

I had now conceived a great desire of returning to England, with a transcript of *The Book of Jasher*, and of the Notes. Hereupon, I and my companions petitioned the commonalty of the city, that we might have the liberty of taking a transcript thereof. Here we were opposed by the treasurer, and our petition was rejected. Some months after this, it came into my mind, that we would petition to have leave to make an English translation of the said Book and Notes. Accordingly, one morning, having drawn up the petition, I sent John of Huntingdon with it, and a wedge of gold to the treasurer, with a letter desiring his opinion of it. After some days, I received for answer, that he had considered of my request, and would shortly relate the affair to the recorder of the city, and take his opinion thereon. Upon this, I despatched Thomas of Malmsbury with a wedge of gold, as a present to the recorder, together with a copy of the petition I had sent the treasurer. A few days after this, I received directions from the recorder, to attend the next court, and then our petition was granted. The order of court ran thus: "We grant unto Alcuin, and his two assistants, full liberty and power of translating out of the original Hebrew, *The Volume of Jasher*, with the Notes appertaining thereto, now contained in a chest in the public library of Gazna, into English, and into no other language whatever. And we likewise order, that the said English translation be made in the library, and in the presence of the custos at such times of the day as shall be most convenient to the said custos."

We soon began the translation in this manner: The manuscript was laid on a table, round which the custos and we sat. The custos opened the volume, and we read the first part or portion, and were permitted to set it down in the original; from whence we made each a translation, and then the custos burnt the part we had so transcribed. And this was the manner in which we proceeded, but the custos would not suffer us to carry home any of our papers.

In fine, after the labour of near a year and six months, we completed the translation of the Book and Notes, to which translation this is prefixed. The treasurer and custos burnt all other papers wrote by either of us, and took from us the translation we had made.

In this dilemma we remained for some time, till, by a proper application, and by petitioning the court a second time, after having been solemnly sworn, that we had taken no other copy, nor were possessed of any other papers, besides that translation of *The Volume of Jasher*, then before the court, the translation was delivered to us, with a charge, that we should not let any person take a copy thereof in any place we passed through in our return to England; which we solemnly promised; and then we were dismissed, with proper credentials for our return through Persia.

We now re-assumed the pilgrims' dress, and after a stay of almost three years, left Gazna, and came to Ispahan, from thence to Casbin, and so back to Rome. Here we stayed some time, and I had an audience of the Pope, when I related to his Holiness, that I had seen *The Book of Jasher,* spoken of in *Joshua,* and in the *Second Book of Samuel.* The holy father, who was now ninety-five years of age, turned to the places I referred to, and then cried out, *I have lived to the days of forgetfulness.*

After a short stay at Rome, we sailed for England, and landed at Bristol, after we had been absent seven years.

VARIOUS READINGS.

Chap. i. ver. 1. IN the head of time.
6. the one that did rule the light, the other that did rule whilst it was dark.
19. and who made the harp and the organ.
20. in his time men began, &c.

Chap. ii. ver. 2. and who ventured to travel, &c.
12. and why should we abolish the customs, &c.

Chap. iii. ver. 2. have deviated from their paths.
10. were at variance.
13. shall inherit after me.
20. Out of thee shall come forth a great nation.
26. a great dearth of grain in that land.
27. was advanced in Egypt.

Chap. v. ver. 8. that opened the womb.

Chap. vi. ver. 7. neither will we bow down to Pharaoh one day more.
9. for he had been gone out of the land, &c.
17. seemed as strangers to Moses.
22. behold our deliverance is in him.

Chap. vii. ver. 8. I never before heard of the sayings of your fathers.

Chap. viii. ver. 13. that I am a messenger to you.
19. had left off to be so.

Chap. ix. ver. 16. And the people were sorely vexed.

Chap. x. ver. 8. The Jacobites יעקבי are not able to fly from us.

Chap. x. ver. 11. wherefore hast thou thus deceitfully undertaken to lead us out of Egypt.
12. unto the enemies of circumcision.
29. between two straits.

Chap. xi. ver. 3. And the sun and the moon gave their light whilst these things were done.

Chap. xii. ver. 18. Seeing ye will not be able to find food for them in the desert.
21. and when we shall depart from hence we know not.

Chap. xiv. v. 2. whom Moses had caused to return.
3. and they pitched their tents at the foot of mount Horeb.
5. this, my daughter Zipporah, thou hast taken to be thy wife.
26. and his name shall stink.
32. shall find useful.

Chap. xvi. ver. 4. even according to the plan Jethro had laid down.

Chap. xvii. v. 2. wise men to hear and speak for you.
20. his spirit was moved within him.

Chap. xviii. v. 7. But Aaron stood aghast.

Chap. xxi. ver. 2. Is not good for the commonweal of Israel.
3. Labour, industry, and painstaking, will they be alien to.
5. Are not all the tribes of Israel sanctified?

VARIOUS READINGS.

Chap. xxi. v. 7. the words of evil you now speak.
10. Depart from Korah, and those that are with him.
14. and they fled every one to his dwelling.

Chap. xxii. v. 4. were familiar with the sons of Israel.

Chap. xxiii. v. 24. the thoughts of the evil one against this people.

Chap. xxiv. v. 4. to bring a description of the land.
6. their dwellings shall you number.
12. Caleb hath the truth in him.

Chap. xxvi. v. 17. That Judah may be many in number.

Chap. xxvii. v. 12. in whom dwelt discernment.
14. Be not angry, O King.
15. Whom thou dost not worship, is on their side.
20. It is the advice of one who has discovered our nakedness.

Chap. xxviii. v. 10. And the bridge.
19. and it became separated to holy uses.
25. put an end to the designs of Achan.

Chap. xxix. v. 2. let no man escape alive.

Chap. xxx. v. 11. Sun, rest thou on Gibeon, and shine thou, moon, on the valley of Ajalon.

Chap. xxxii. v. 4. Cut off the flesh of thy foreskin, then shalt thou beget a son.
7. Take sharp knives.
10. after he cometh out of the womb.

Chap. xxxiii. v. 8. and let them ask of them the reason for their so doing.
9. and behold they were well pleasing to the eye.
11. Wherefore have ye built this tabernacle and this altar? Surely to defy Joshua and the elders of Israel.
17. turned away the anger of Phinehas, &c.

Chap. xxxiv. v. 7. were too strong for them.
10. Who can command the Reubenites, the Gadites, and all the people of Israel, to go up to the war.

Chap. xxxv. v. 2. Who shall be judge in Israel?
18. then should we be able to drive out the nations.

Chap. xxxvi. v. 5. It seemeth well unto me, that ye gather yourselves together at Bethel, that I, and the elders of Israel, may make an agreement with you.

Chap. xxxvii. v. 16. And there was a great want of grain in Canaan.
17. seated Joseph on his right hand.

¶ THE BOOK OF

JASHER.[I]

I *Heb.* THE UPRIGHT.

CHAP. I.

1 *The formation of the world.* 3 *the light shineth.* 7 *the earth is productive.* 11 *the creation of man.* 13 *the birth of Cain and Abel.* 17 *of Enoch.* 23 *the death of Adam.*

A. M. 1.

1 WHILST it was the [a] beginning, darkness overspread the face of [b]nature.

2 And the [c]ether moved upon the surface of the [d]chaos.

3 And it came to pass, that a great [e]light shone forth from the firmament, and enlightened the [f]abyss.

4 And the abyss fled before the face of the light, and divided between the light and the darkness.

5 So that the face of nature was formed a second time.

6 And behold there appeared in the firmament two great lights: the one to rule the light, and the other to rule the darkness.

7 And the [g]ground brought forth grass: the herb yielding seed, and the fruit-tree after his kind.

8 And every beast after his kind: and every thing that creepeth, after their kind.

9 And the waters brought forth the moving creatures, after their kind.

10 And the ether brought forth every winged fowl, after his kind.

11 ¶ And when all these things were [h]fulfilled, behold [i] JEHOVAH appeared in [k]Eden, and created man, and made him to be an [l]image of his own eternity.

12 And to him was given power and [m] lordship over all living creatures, and over every herb, and over every tree of the field.

13 And it came to pass, in process of time, that the man begat [n]Cain: and he also begat his brother [o]Abel.

14 And Cain was the first man who tilled the ground:

A. M. 1.

[a] *Heb.* the prime
[b] *Heb.* the desert
[c] *Heb.* the atoms
[d] *Heb.* confused mass of matter.
[e] *Heb.* the flame, *or*, burning.
[f] *Heb.* the bottomless pit.
[g] *Heb.* the earth, *or*, nature.
[h] *Heb.* finished.
[i] *Heb.* I am that I am.
[k] *Heb.* delighted
[l] *Heb.* likeness.
[m] *Heb.* rule.
[n] *Heb.* the possessed.
[o] *Heb.* the feeder

A. M. 61. 15 And Abel was a feeder
of sheep.

16 And Cain went out and
dwelt on the east of Eden, in
the land of [p]Nod.

[p] *Heb.* peregrination.

17 And Cain begat [q]Enoch:
then did men begin to build
cities.

[q] *Heb.* the civilized.

18 And unto [r]Lamech was
born [s]Jabal: he was the
first who taught men to build
tents.

[r] *Heb.* the meanspirited.
[s] *Heb.* the experienced.

19 And unto Lamech also
was born [t]Tubal-Cain: he was
the first who wrought in brass
and iron, and who builded up
the [u]harp and the organ.

[t] *Heb.* the emulous.
[u] *Heb.* all kinds of music.

20 And [x]Seth begat
[y]Enos: then began men
by name to call on the
Lord.

[x] *Heb.* the regular.
[y] *Heb.* the despondent.

21 And all the days of the
life of [z]Adam, there was rest,
and peace, and quiet, unto all
men.

[z] *Heb.* the flesh.

22 For they listened unto
all things, concerning which
he spake unto them.

930. 23 And Adam lived nine
hundred and thirty years, and
he died.

CHAP. II.

1 *The birth of Noah.* 2 *he first buildeth the ship.* 4 *all the people speak one language.* 8 *Noah dies.* 10 *Peleg is born.* 11 *he divideth the land.* 13 *Nimrod opposeth Peleg, and the people are dispersed.*

1056. 1 AND Lamech, the son of
[a]Methuselah, begat
[b]Noah.

[a] *Heb.* the soil of death.
[b] *Heb.* rest.

2 And Noah was the first A. M. 1537.
who builded the ship: and
who sojourned upon the great
waters.

3 And he was the father of
those who go down into the
deep, and who occupy them-
selves in much water.

4 At this time the whole 1757.
was of one [c]lip, and of one
word: and there was peace
unto all.

[c] *Heb.* tongue.

5 ¶ And it came to pass,
that men were multiplied be-
fore the face of the earth; and
they became mighty, and men
of renown.

6 And [d]Japhet, and his
sons, and his sons' sons, said
unto Noah, Behold, thou art
our [e]father! permit us, we
beseech thee, seeing the land
is not able to bear us, our chil-
dren, and our herds, and our
flocks, to pass over and dwell
in the plain of [f]Shinar.

[d] *Heb.* the persuader.
[e] *Heb.* ruler.
[f] *Heb.* vigilance

7 And Noah said, Be it
unto you, as ye list: only this
thing I command ye, that ye
worship the God of your fa-
thers, observing all things
which ye have received.

8 And Noah lived nine hun- 2010.
dred and thirty years: and he
died.

9 And from these men of
renown rose up great nations,
by whom the isles of the [g]Gen-
tiles were peopled.

[g] *Or,* strangers

10 ¶ And it came to pass, 1729.
in process of time, that there
stood up among men, [h]Peleg,
the son of [i]Eber.

[h] *Heb.* the divider.
[i] *Heb.* the wrathful.

A. M. 1750.

11 It was he who first invented the hedge and ditch, the wall and bulwark: and who by lot divided the lands among his brethren.

12 And [k] Nimrod said, Wherefore should we obey Peleg: and why should we forsake the customs of our forefathers.

[k] *Heb.* the headstrong.

13 And the people hearkened unto him: for Nimrod was a mighty hunter, and a man of renown.

14 And there arose a great strife among the people: and they were scattered upon the earth.

15 And Nimrod builded him cities: and he gathered together the scattered of the land.

CHAP. III.

1 *Abraham and Sarah.* 4 *he leaves Canaan.* 6 *goes into Egypt.* 8 *his riches.* 11 *removes to Mamre,* 16 *circumcises himself.* 20 *Sarah dissuades him from slaying his son Isaac.* 39 *his death.* 41 *Isaac dies.* 43 *a famine in Canaan.* 48 *Pharaoh sends for Jacob into Egypt.* 51 *Jacob goes.* 53 *his death*

2093.

1 AND [a]Abraham was the son of [b] Terah: and [c]Sarah was the wife of Abraham.

[a] *Heb.* the multitude.
[b] *Heb.* the discontented.
[c] *Heb.* the fruitful.

2 And Abraham said, Lo, the nations are full of confusion: and the inhabitants of the earth have perverted their ways.

3 Thus saith Abraham, the son of Terah, I have spied iniquity among the Gentiles, and evil among the sons of Cain. A. M. 2098.

4 And Abraham departed from his brethren, and passed through the land of [d] Canaan, he and his wife; and he pitched his tent on the plain of [e]Moriah.

[d] *Heb.* delightful.
[e] *Heb.* morose.

5 And as he journeyed still on to the south, he heard a voice saying unto him, [f] I will make of thee a great nation.

[f] *Heb.* Out of thee shall come forth a great nation.

6 ¶ And Abraham went into [g] Egypt: and he abode there, and found favour with [h] Pharaoh.

[g] *Heb.* bondage.
[h] *Heb.* the unwilling.

7 And Pharaoh gave unto Abraham, sheep and oxen: and he-asses and she-asses, and men-servants and maid-servants.

8 And Abraham was rich in cattle, and in men-servants and maid-servants, and in silver and gold: and Abraham went up out of Egypt, even unto [i] Bethel did he go.

[i] *Heb.* house of God.

9 And the herds and possessions of Abraham increased exceedingly: so that the [k] land was not able to bear them.

[k] *Heb.* spot.

10 Insomuch that the servants of Abraham, and the servants of [l] Lot strove together.

[l] *Heb.* the distressed.

11 Then Abraham arose, his wife, his servants, and his flocks: and he removed his tent, and he came and dwelt

A. M. 2103.

in the plain of [m]Mamre, nigh unto [n]Hebron.

[m] *Heb.* rebellion
[n] *Heb.* charm.

12 ¶ Now so it came to pass, that Sarah, Abraham's wife, had not brought forth her first-born.

13 And Abraham complained, and said; Unto me thou hast not given an heir: lo! the stranger, born in my house, shall rule after me.

14 And Abraham heard a voice saying unto him, Circumcise the flesh of thy foreskin, for therefore art thou barren.

15 And Abraham did so: and he went in unto Sarah, and she conceived, and bare a son, and he called his name [o]Isaac.

[o] *Heb.* the laugh

16 And Abraham was ninety and nine years old, when he circumcised the flesh of his foreskin.

17 And Abraham removed from the plains of Mamre, and went and dwelt between [p]Kadesh and [q]Shur.

[p] *Heb.* holy.
[q] *Heb.* strong.

18 And Abraham was stricken in years, and his strength failed him.

19 And when Isaac was twenty and five years old, Abraham heard a voice, saying, Take thy son, and slay him, and offer him up a burnt-offering in the land wherein he was born.

20 And Sarah spake unto Abraham, and said, The holy voice hath not so spoken; for remember thou the words of that voice which said unto thee, I will make of thee a great nation.

A. M. 2144.

21 [¶ And Abraham rose up early in the morning, and saddled his ass, and took two of his young men with him, and Isaac his son, and clave the wood for the burnt-offering, and rose up, and went unto the place of which God had told him.

22 Then on the third day Abraham lifted up his eyes, and saw the place afar off.

23 And Abraham said unto his young men, Abide ye here with the ass; and I and the lad will go yonder and worship, and come again to you.

24 And Abraham took the wood of the burnt-offering, and laid it upon Isaac his son; and he took the fire in his hand, and a knife; and they went both of them together.

25 And Isaac spake unto Abraham his father, and said, My father: and he said, Here am I, my son. And he said, Behold the fire and the wood: but where is the lamb for a burnt-offering?

26 And Abraham said, My son, God will provide himself a lamb for a burnt-offering: so they went both of them together.

27 And they came to the place which God had told him of; and Abraham built an altar there, and laid the wood in order, and bound Isaac his son,

A. M. and laid him on the altar upon the wood.

28 And Abraham stretched forth his hand, and took the knife to slay his son.

29 And the angel of the Lord called unto him out of heaven, and said, Abraham, Abraham: and he said, Here am I.

30 And he said, Lay not thy hand upon the lad, neither do thou any thing unto him: for now I know that thou fearest God, seeing thou hast not withheld thy son, thine only son from me.

31 And Abraham lifted up his eyes, and looked, and behold behind him a ram caught in a thicket by his horns: and Abraham went and took the ram, and offered him up for a burnt-offering in the stead of his son.

32 And Abraham called the name of that place Jehovah-jireh: as it is said to this day, In the mount of the Lord it shall be seen.

33 ¶ And the angel of the Lord called unto Abraham out of heaven the second time,

34 And said, By myself have I sworn, saith the Lord, for because thou hast done this thing, and hast not withheld thy son, thine only son:

35 That in blessing I will bless thee, and in multiplying I will multiply thy seed as the stars of the heaven, and as the sand which is upon the sea
shore; and thy seed shall pos- A. M.
sess the gate of his enemies. 2144.

36 And in thy seed shall all the nations of the earth be blessed; because thou hast obeyed my voice.

37 So Abraham returned unto his young men, and they rose up and went together to Beer-sheba; and Abraham dwelt at Beer-sheba.]

38 And Abraham repented him of the evil he purposed to do unto his son, his only son, Isaac.

39 And Abraham died, and 2190.
was buried; even in the place where Sarah his wife was buried, there was he buried also.

40 ¶ And Isaac begat [r] Jacob of [s] Rebecca his wife.

[r] Heb. the supplanter.
[s] Heb. the glutted.

41 And it came to pass, in process of time, that Isaac was gathered unto his fathers: and Jacob increased in men-servants, and in maid-servants, and in sheep, and in oxen, in he-asses and in she-asses, and in silver and in gold.

42 And Jacob dwelt in the land of Canaan.

43 ¶ And it came to pass, 2292.
after many days were fulfilled, that there was a great famine in that land.

44 And [t] Joseph, one of the sons of Jacob, in those days ministered in Egypt.

[t] Heb. the added

45 And Jacob said unto his sons, Arise, go down into Egypt, and buy ye corn for us, your wives, and your little ones, that we and they may live, and not die.

A. M. 2299.

46 And they saddled their asses, and they journeyed into Egypt, and they hastened to do according to all that Jacob had spoken, for the famine was sore in the land.

47 And Joseph interceded for his brethren: and Pharaoh said unto the sons of Jacob, Lade ye your beasts, and return ye into the land of Canaan.

48 And say ye unto your father, Thus saith Pharaoh, king of Egypt, Come unto me, ye, your wives, your sons, and your daughters, and your little ones; and ye shall dwell in the land of Egypt, and ye shall eat of the [u]fat of the land.

[u] *Heb.* the best food.

49 And they returned into Canaan; and they told unto Jacob, their father, all those things which Pharaoh had commanded them.

50 And Jacob accepted the offer that Pharaoh had made him, because the famine was sore in the land of Canaan.

51 And Jacob delayed not, but came down, he, and his family, into Egypt.

52 And Pharaoh gave him the land of [x]Goshen to dwell in, which was near.

[x] *Heb.* nigh.

2315. 53 And Jacob died in the land of Goshen, in the land of Egypt.

CHAP. IV.

2 *The Israelites increase.* 4 *They want to go into Canaan.* 6 *Pharaoh will not let them go.* 13 *Zapnah's counsel.* 20 *The Israelites are taxed.*

A. M. 2335.

1 AND the children of Israel sojourned in the land of Egypt many years after the death of Jacob their father.

2 And it came to pass in process of time, that they increased abundantly, and they waxed mighty; and the land of Goshen was filled with them.

3 And they sent messengers unto Pharaoh, king of Egypt, saying:

4 The land in which we dwell is not able to bear us, our children, our flocks, and our cattle; wherefore we pray thee, suffer us to return into the land of Canaan from whence we came out.

5 And Pharaoh said unto his servants, even unto the wise men of his kingdom:

6 How is this, that the children of Jacob say unto us, Suffer us to return into the land of Canaan from whence we came out?

7 Are they not the subjects of the Egyptians? have we not bought them with a price?

8 And the wise men answered Pharaoh, and said: When the famine was sore in the land of Canaan, thy father's father gave unto Jacob and his children the land of Goshen for to dwell in, and with the fat of Egypt were they sustained.

9 Now, know, O king, in those days, thy father's father advanced one Joseph, an [a]He-

[a] *Heb.* the alien.

A. M. brew, who was the son of
2375. [b]Jacob.
10 And he was a stranger
in the land of Egypt; and he
bought Egypt with a price.
11 And Pharaoh said, have
we nourished them, and shall
they [c]now turn up the heel
against us?
12 And [d]Zapnah stood
forth and said: Hearken unto
me, O Pharaoh, king of
Egypt, let thy servant speak,
let the words of my mouth
find favour before thee.
13 And Zapnah said, The
children of Jacob are become
a great people for number;
and they increase daily, and
they thirst after dominion.
14 And peradventure it shall
come to pass that they shall
[e]join themselves unto our enemies,
and fight against us, and
slay us, and take away from us
our inheritance.
15 Send therefore unto Goshen,
even unto the children
of Jacob, saying, Ye shall
number the males according
to your tribes, from him that
is able to go forth to battle,
even to the hoary head; the
females also ye shall number,
ye shall number the children
of Jacob both males and females.
16 And Pharaoh did so:
and Pharaoh said: Behold the
sons of Jacob are more in
number than my own people.
17 Up now, let us set over
them task-masters; for the

[b] *Heb.* the exactor.
[c] *Heb.* rebel.
[d] *Chald.* the hard.
[e] *Heb.* go in.

land of Egypt groaneth, it is A. M.
heavy laden, it bendeth under 2377.
its burthen.
18 Now the land of Egypt
gave of its increase unto Pharaoh,
the fifth part thereof.
19 And Pharaoh said: Of
the increase of the land of
Egypt shall ye every year
bring into my storehouses, the
tenth part thereof.
20 And of the increase of
the land of Goshen shall the
children of Jacob bring unto
[f]Pithom and [g]Raamses year by
year the tenth part thereof,
without waste shall they bring
it.
21 So the Egyptians were
eased of their burthens; and
the children of Israel were
grievously oppressed.
22 ¶ All these things which
I Jasher have written, received
I from [h]Caleb my father, yea,
even from [i]Hezron my father's
father, and from [k]Azuba who
travailed with me.

CHAP. V.

4 Pharaoh again oppresses the Israelites. 6 He orders the males of the Hebrews to be killed. 8 Moses is born. 13 Pharaoh's daughter intercedeth for the Hebrew males. 14 Moses becomes her son.

1 THESE are the words of
Jasher, the son of Caleb, 2385.
by Azuba.
2 And it came to pass in
process of time, that the children
of [a]Israel were multiplied
exceedingly.

[f] *Heb.* accomplished.
[g] *Heb.* threatening.
[h] *Heb.* the hearty.
[i] *Heb.* the arrow of joy.
[k] *Heb.* the chaste.
[a] *Heb.* prevailing.

A. M. 2395.

3 And they said one unto the other, Shall we bow down and serve the Egyptians, seeing we are become more, and mightier than they.

4 And the sayings of the children of Israel were told unto Pharaoh; and he said, They are wanton, they lift up the heel; set over them more task-masters.

5 And they did so; but it availed not: for the more the house of Jacob was afflicted, the more they increased and multiplied.

6 And Pharaoh was greatly vexed, and he said, This people will eat us up; wherefore ye shall slay every male of the Hebrews that cometh out of the womb, in the day that he is born shall he surely die.

7 Now when the daughter of Pharaoh heard of these things she sought to turn away the evil imaginations of her father against the males of the children of Israel.

8 And it came to pass that [b]Moses the son of [c]Amram, by [d]Jochebed his wife, was the first male that came out of the womb after the decree of Pharaoh, king of Egypt, to slay all the males of the Hebrews.

[b] *Heb.* drawn from the water. [c] *Heb.* the robust. [d] *Heb.* the comely.

9 And Jochebed the mother of Moses, with [e]Miriam his sister, came unto Pharaoh's daughter; and Jochebed said, Behold here the son of thy handmaid!

[e] *Heb.* the praiser.

A. M. 2433.

10 And Pharaoh's daughter said, What wist you?

11 And they said, Thy father hath commanded that this infant be slain; yea, and that all the Hebrew males as soon as they are born be slain also.

12 And Pharaoh's daughter said, Give unto me the child. And they did so. And she said, This shall be my son.

13 And it came to pass, that the wrath of Pharaoh was turned away from slaying the males of the Hebrews.

14 And the child Moses grew and increased in stature, and was learned in all the magic of the Egyptians.

CHAP. VI.

3 *Moses leaves Egypt, and goes into Goshen.* 5 *Proposes to his brethren to shake off the Egyptian yoke.* 8 *Pharaoh hears of this.* 10 *Moses flies into Midiam.* 12 *Caleb invents the bow.* 14 *Moses comes into Goshen.* 18 *The Hebrews reprove Moses.* 21 *Their burdens.*

1 AND it came to pass in those days, that Pharaoh died; and the daughter of Pharaoh died also.

2 And there arose up a king who knew not Moses; neither regarded he the children of Israel.

3 ¶ When all these things were accomplished, Moses 2473.
came up out of Egypt; and he sojourned with his brethren in the land of Goshen.

A. M. 2473. 4 And Moses saw the oppression of the Egyptians, wherewith they oppressed his brethren: and it grieved him to the heart.

5 And he said unto his brethren, Let us shake off the yoke of the Egyptians: let us cast away their bondage from us.

6 We be more in number than the people of Egypt, the lesser should always bow down and serve the greater: as it is written in the prophecy of Jacob our father.

7 The fifth part of the increase of our lands will we not give the Egyptians: neither will we serve Pharaoh any longer.

8 Now when it was told Pharaoh, That Moses stirred up the people: and made them uneasy under their burthens;

9 That Pharaoh sent messengers unto Moses, but they found him not: for he had fled out of the land of Goshen from the face of Pharaoh, into the land of [a]Midian.

[a] *Heb.* judging.

10 And Moses abode with [b]Jethro, the prince of Midian: and Moses took to wife, [c]Zipporah, the daughter of Jethro. And he dwelt with him thirty and nine years.

[b] *Heb.* the excellent.
[c] *Heb.* the cause of contention.

11 ¶ And it came to pass
after Moses had fled from the
2488. face of Pharaoh, and had left
his brethren in the land of
Goshen,

A. M. 2488. 12 That Caleb, the son of Hezron, invented the bow: for he was a mighty man, and a man of renown.

13 He taught the children of Jacob to shoot with the bow: he learnt his brethren to prepare themselves for the battle.

14 ¶ And Moses was eigh- 2512.
ty years old: and it was told
unto him, saying, Pharaoh
who sought thy life is dead.

15 And Moses sent [e]Gershom his son before his face: and Moses came, he and his wife, into the land of Goshen, even to his brethren did he come.

[e] *Heb.* the peregrine.

16 And Moses spake unto the children of Israel, and said, Whilst I sojourned in the land of Midian, I heard a voice saying unto me: Arise, go up unto thy brethren, for I will by thy hand bring back the children of Jacob, and they shall possess the land of Canaan from whence they came out.

17 And the elders of the children of Israel knew not Moses: neither regarded they the words of his mouth.

18 And they said unto Moses, Thou hast polluted the house of Jacob: for lo! thou hast taken to wife one who is not an Israelite.

19 And Moses said: [f]I have sinned.

[f] *Or,* I have deviated.

20 And Moses put away Zipporah and her children:

A. M. 2513.

and they returned unto Jethro in the land of Midian.

21 ¶Then stood forth Caleb and said, The Egyptians have laid on us great weights, burthens that we are not able to bear, and the necks of the people are sore through the pressure thereof;

22 Let us therefore hearken unto the words of Moses; peradventure salvation is on his right hand.

23 For this fifty years have we served with great toil the Egyptians, with the sweat of our brows we have borne heavy burthens, and they have not touched them with the little finger.

24 And Moses said, Trust in the Lord God of your fathers, for he will bring you up out of the affliction wherewith the Egyptians oppress you, unto the land of our father Jacob, unto a land flowing with milk and honey.

25 A land whereon my feet have stood, and mine eyes have seen:

26 That ye may be a great people, a people whose number may be as the stars in the firmament, and as the sand upon the sea-shore.

27 Wherefore I will go unto Pharaoh, peradventure he will let the children of Israel go up out of the land of Egypt unto the land of Canaan, even unto the heritage of our forefathers.

CHAP. VII.

A. M. 2513.

2 Moses goes unto Pharaoh. 6 Desires that he might lead the Hebrews into the land of Canaan. 10 Pharaoh straightens the Hebrews. 16 They are angry with Moses and Aaron.

1 AND it came to pass, when the people saw all the signs and the wonders which Moses wrought in the sight of all Israel, in the presence of the congregation, that they believed.

2 And Moses said unto the elders of Israel, Send also with me [a]Aaron, my brother, that he may be a spokesman for me, and for you.

[a] Heb. the eloquent.

3 And also Jasher, the son of Caleb, that he may bear the rod before us.

4 And the elders of Israel said unto Aaron, and unto Jasher, Go, and may ye, and all the children of Jacob, find favour in the sight of Pharaoh, king of Egypt.

5 Then went Moses unto Pharaoh, and said, Fourscore and one years have we served thee, yea, with rigorous servitude have bowed down our necks unto thee.

6 And behold the land of Goshen is not able to bear us; the number of thy servants increase daily, wherefore, let us now pass through the land of Egypt unto the wilderness, that we may go and sojourn in the land of Canaan, from whence we came out.

A. M. 2513.

7 For behold, O Pharaoh! thus hath said our forefathers, Abraham, Isaac, and Jacob: The land of Canaan shall be thine inheritance, it shall be the dwelling of your sons, your sons' sons, and your posterity for ever.

8 And Pharaoh said, Are ye come hither to mock me? I regard not the prophecies of your fathers, neither will I let the children of Israel go up out of the land.

9 The house of Jacob are the nurture of the Egyptians: wherefore do ye, Moses and Aaron, dissuade the people from their duty.

10 ¶ Then Pharaoh called unto him the task-masters, whom he had set over the children of Israel, and he said unto them, Ye are negligent; bring ye unto my treasure-cities, Pithom and Raamses, the fifth of the increase of the land of Goshen, by the sixth day, ye shall bring it to the full tale thereof.

11 And the task-masters did as Pharaoh had commanded; and they pressed sore the officers of the children of Israel.

12 And they were straightened for time, because the commandment of Pharaoh was urgent.

13 And they cried unto Pharaoh, and said, Give unto thy servants other six days, so shall we be able to obey thy voice, O Pharaoh!

14 But Pharaoh answered, I will not, hasten therefore, and bring of the increase of your lands, your flocks, and your herds, even the fifth part of them shall ye bring unto Pithom and Raamses.

15 And as they departed, the officers of the children of Israel met Moses and Aaron in the way, and they said unto them,

16 Pharaoh will not hear us, neither regardeth he the words of our forefathers, neither hath the words of you, Moses and Aaron, any power over him, it had been better for us you had never gone forth and spake unto him.

17 And Moses was angry because of the sayings of the officers of the children of Israel, and Moses said,

18 Wherefore should Pharaoh evil intreat the children of Israel?

A. M. 2513.

CHAP. VIII.

2 *Moses persuades the people to go out of Egypt.* 8 *Goes again to Pharaoh.* 12 *Moses's rod.* 17 *Becomes a serpent.* 23 *Turns the river into blood.* 25 *The river brings forth frogs.* 30 *Pharaoh will not let the Hebrews go.*

1 AND it came to pass on the morrow, that Moses assembled together the sons of [a]Reuben, [b]Simeon, [c]Levi, [d]Gershon, [e]Kohath, [f]Merari, [g]Izhar, [h]Uzziel, and [i]Korah,

[a] *Heb.* I have seen my son.
[b] *Heb.* the attentive.
[c] *Heb.* coupled.
[d] *Heb.* the stranger.
[e] *Heb.* gathering.
[f] bitter.
[g] *Heb.* bright.
[h] *Heb.* the strength of God.
[i] *Heb.* bald.

A. M. 2513.

even the heads of the families of the children of Israel.

2 And Moses said unto them, The heart of Pharaoh is set against us, and it cometh to pass, when we speak unto him to go three days' journey into the wilderness, that he oppresseth us sore.

3 And now, O elders of Israel, ye this day bear me witness, how that our fathers, even Abraham, Isaac, and Jacob, dwelt in the land of Canaan, and possessed the same.

4 And they said unto us, It is a land that floweth with milk and honey.

5 And this we ourselves know, that the compass of it will receive us, our wives, our children, and our flocks.

6 Remember also the words which Jacob spake unto us, when as yet he was with us: Ye shall go up and dwell in the land of your fathers.

7 And the heads of the families of the children of Israel said unto Moses: Go unto Pharaoh in our names, in the names of the elders of the house of Jacob.

8 ¶ And Moses went unto Pharaoh: and Pharaoh was walking in his garden, by the river side, and his wise men were with him.

9 And Moses said unto Pharaoh, Let us, we pray thee, go through the land of Egypt unto the wilderness, that we may serve the Lord.

10 And Pharaoh answered and said: Surely to make a nation of thy people, that thou mayest rule over them, art thou come! From whence art thou? A. M. 2513.

11 And Moses spake unto Pharaoh, and said, The Lord hath sent me: out of Midian am I come.

12 And Pharaoh said unto Moses, What meanest that rod that is borne before you, Moses, and before you, Aaron?

13 And Moses spake out aloud unto Pharaoh, and said, Thus saith the Lord: It is the wand and token of my power, whereby you, and all the Egyptians shall know, that I am sent unto you.

14 And Pharaoh was seated under a pavilion, he and his wise men: and Moses, Aaron, and Jasher, stood there also.

15 And Pharaoh said, Is that the rod of which I have been told, that thou, Moses, didst throw it upon the earth, before the elders of Israel, and it became as a serpent?

16 And Moses said, O Pharaoh! it came to pass as thou hast spoken.

17 And the heart of Pharaoh was as salt: and Moses took the rod, and he threw it down before Pharaoh, and before his servants, and the rod became as a serpent.

18 Then the wise men, the magicians, and sorcerers of Egypt, threw down their rods

A. M. 2513.

before Pharaoh: and their rods became as serpents.

19 But the rod of Moses was as a serpent, when the rods of the magicians and sorcerers were not so.

20 ¶ And it came to pass on the morning of the next day, as Pharaoh walked by the river side, Moses spake unto Pharaoh, and said,

21 Lo! this will I do; I will smite this river, which thou seest, with this rod, and the water thereof shall become as blood, and all the moving creatures therein shall die, and the river shall stink.

22 And Pharaoh said unto Moses, If thou canst do this thing, thou art able to be a lawgiver to, and a ruler over thy people.

23 And Moses smote the river with his rod, and the river was as blood: and the magicians did so.

24 And Pharaoh laughed at Moses.

25 ¶ And it came to pass on the morrow, that Moses smote the river, and it brought forth frogs in abundance, so that they crawled upon the banks thereof.

26 And the magicians and sorcerers of Egypt with their rods smote the river, and it brought forth frogs.

27 And Pharaoh spake unto Moses, and said: Where are now thy wonders, seeing my servants do the like?

28 And Moses went out from before the face of Pharaoh. A. M. 2513.

29 ¶ And Moses returned into the land of Goshen, and he called for the elders of Israel: and he told them all that he had done in Egypt.

30 And that Pharaoh would not let them from their burthens to go through the land of Egypt into the land of Canaan, as our fathers had promised unto us, and unto our seed for ever.

CHAP. IX.

1 *Caleb proposes to fight their way through Egypt,* 9 *which is told Pharaoh,* 11 *who is willing to let them go on certain conditions.* 19 *the Hebrews sell their possessions to the Egyptians,* 23 *whom they spoil.* 26 *the Hebrews go out armed.*

1 AND in those days it came to pass, that Caleb, the son of Hezron, stood up before the assembly of the children of Israel, and he said unto them:

2 Now know ye, that Pharaoh and his servants will not let us go peaceably through Egypt unto the promised land.

3 Are the Egyptians to compare with us? Can they bend the bow? Can they set forth the battle?

4 Are not they backsliders? Are they not weak? Do not they delight in ease and in soft raiment?

A. M. 2513.

5 Wherefore thus saith Caleb, the son of Hezron: Up, let us take the bow, and on the morrow let us enter the land of Egypt to pass through it to the land of our father Jacob.

6 And let no man do hurt unto the Egyptians, unless Pharaoh and his servants should seek to slay us.

7 And the counsel of Caleb was pleasing unto all the disciples of the bow, who were the followers of the son of Hezron.

8 And Moses said, Caleb, the son of Hezron, hath well spoken: By midnight on the morrow, will we and all the host of Israel assay to go up out of the land of Egypt.

9 ¶ And it came to pass on the morrow, that these things were told unto Pharaoh, and unto those that were with him.

10 And the wise men of Egypt said unto Pharaoh, Let the Hebrews go, lest peradventure they slay us, our wives, and our children, and take away the land from us.

11 Then Pharaoh called for Moses, and for all the elders of the children of Israel, and he said unto them, I will let you, your wives, and your children go: only your flocks and your herds, they you shall leave behind; so shall you go up out of the land.

12 And Moses said, How then shall the people be sustained as they pass through Egypt, and when they come into the wilderness, if our flocks and our herds go not with us.

A. M. 2513.

13 And Pharaoh said, As you pass through the land of Egypt, I will command my servants, and they shall lodge you by night, and provide food for you by day.

14 Wherefore shall ye leave your flocks, and your herds, and the increase of your lands, behind ye: then shall ye pass through the land of Egypt. and no one shall fight against you.

15 Seeing if you lead your flocks and your herds into the wilderness, there must they perish in the desert.

16 And Moses went forth from Pharaoh, and spake unto the children of Israel, saying, Pharaoh will let us go, our wives and our children, but our flocks and our herds, and the increase of our lands must we leave behind us in the land of Goshen. And the people were moved.

17 ¶ Then spake Moses and the elders of Israel unto Pharaoh, and said, Thy people shall buy our flocks, and our herds, and the increase of our lands with a price, that we may have wherewith to purchase necessaries of thy servants, the Egyptians, as we pass through thy land.

18 And Pharaoh said, Now will I let the people go, only

A. M. 2513. this shall you observe, That my people shall give you for your flocks, and for your cattle, and for the increase of your lands, such pieces of money as they shall think proper, and you shall sell unto them all your possessions.

19 And Moses and the elders sold unto the Egyptians on a set-day, even all that they had, their cattle, their houses, the fruit of the ground, yea, all the worth of the children of Israel.

20 Only Miriam begged of the Egyptians a male and a female of every flock, and of every herd, and of every fowl, and of every beast.

21 ¶And it came to pass, that the flocks, and the herds, and the possessions of the children of Israel were so great in number, that the Egyptians lacked money to make good the purchase thereof.

22 And the Egyptians said unto their wives, and unto their daughters, give unto us your ear-rings, your jewels of silver, and your jewels of gold, that we may pay unto the Hebrews that which we owe unto them.

23 And the price thereof spoiled the Egyptians.

24 ¶And it came to pass, when the sale was over, that Moses hastened the children of Israel to go up out of the land of Egypt.

25 And the trumpet sounded about midnight, and the children of Israel hastened with great haste to go up out of Egypt. A. M. 2513.

26 And Caleb spake in the ears of the people, and he said, Let every man take his bow in his hand; so shall Israel go up out of the land of bondage with an out-stretched arm.

27 And they did so: and great fear fell upon all the Egyptians.

CHAP. X.

1 *The Hebrews deceive the Egyptians.* 5 *Pharaoh pursues them.* 11 *The Israelites murmur against Moses.* 15 *The people send Jasher to Pharaoh.* 30 *Resolve to pass the Red Sea.*

1 NOW it came to pass on the morrow, that the Egyptians began to count the flocks, and the herds, and the possessions of the children of Israel, which they had sold unto the Egyptians, and behold there lacked in the tale thereof.

2 Then the people of Egypt cried unto Pharaoh, and said: We have done wrong in letting the children of Jacob our nurture go away from serving thee and thy people.

3 For lo! the Hebrews have sold unto us more in number of their flocks and their herds, and their possessions than they had.

4 And Pharaoh said, Arise, let us pursue after them, per-

A. M. 2513.

adventure we shall overtake them before they have gotten into the wilderness.

5 And Pharaoh and the Egyptians pursued after the children of Israel: even unto [a]Ethem in the wilderness, at the extremity of the Red Sea.

6 ¶ Now it came to pass, when Moses perceived that Pharaoh pursued after the Israelites by the way of the wilderness, that he turned off, and he and all Israel came unto [b]Baal-zephon, which is on this side of the Red Sea.

7 And it was told unto Pharaoh, that Moses and the Hebrews had fled by the way of Baal-zephon.

8 Then said Pharaoh unto his captains, and unto the rulers of his host: Lo! the host of Egypt waxeth slack, let us remain here for some time, and let us send forth spies; for behold! the deceivers cannot escape out of our hands.

9 And Moses sent messengers unto Pharaoh, saying, Wherefore follow ye after us? Are not the tribes of Israel in number more than the people of Egypt? Let us go and serve the Lord in the wilderness, we pray thee!

10 And Pharaoh answered those that were sent unto him, and said, Because ye have deceived Pharaoh and his servants: because ye have spoiled the Egyptians. And Pharaoh was exceeding wroth.

11 And the children of Israel cried unto Moses, and said, Wherefore hast thou attempted thus vainly to bring us up out of Egypt, Surely, as sheep appointed for the slaughter are we come!

12 ¶ Then stood forth Caleb and said, Let every man take his bow in his hand: for it is far better that a few of us die, than that we, our wives, our children, our gold, and our silver, should fall a sacrifice unto the uncircumcised.

13 Remember how the Egyptians evilly intreated us: let us not forget the burthens which we have borne.

14 And the people cried out with one voice, We will die here: or we will slay the Egyptians.

15 Then Moses, Aaron, and the elders of Israel, sent Jasher unto Pharaoh, saying:

16 Behold, thus saith Moses, Aaron, and all the elders of Israel, On the morrow, by the break of day, we will restore unto thy people, if so be it shall be found that we have done wrong unto the people of Egypt, thy servants.

17 And Pharaoh said unto Jasher, Say thou unto Moses, unto Aaron, and unto the elders of the children of Israel, that, I, Pharaoh, will abide in this place, and all the host of the Egyptians.

18 But if on the morrow, Moses, Aaron, and the elders

A. M. 2513.

[a] *Heb.* strong.

[b] *Heb.* secreted.

A. M. 2513. of Israel shall delay to perform the covenant they have this day made, then will I and all the host of Egypt follow after them, and slay them: none shall escape; no, not one.

19 And when Jasher had heard all that Pharaoh spake unto him: then returned he unto Moses, unto Aaron, and unto the elders of Israel, and he said unto them;

20 Thus saith Pharaoh, I, Pharaoh, will abide in this place, and all the host of the Egyptians.

21 But if on the morrow, Moses, Aaron, and the elders of Israel shall delay to perform the covenant they have this day made, then will I and all the host of Egypt follow after them, and slay them: none shall escape; no, not one.

22 And the people feared greatly; because they had spoiled the Egyptians.

23 ¶ Then Moses called unto the people, and said, Behold! there is left unto us but one way, whereby we may escape the [c]anger of Pharaoh: and of those that are with him.

[c] *Heb.* the fury.

24 It is now midnight, and by the time of the cock-crow the Red Sea will be dried up: and peradventure we may cross over dry-shod into the wilderness.

25 And it shall come to pass, that if Pharaoh and his host shall assay to come after us, the waters shall return and overwhelm them.

A. M. 2513.

26 Then Moses commanded Aaron, saying, About the mid of night, ye shall pass through the Red Sea, you and the people who lie on the bank thereof: ye shall pass through, until all have passed through.

27 And after that, I and the people that shall remain with me will pass through the Red Sea.

28 And Pharaoh and the Egyptians shall not know of our departure, until the hindermost have entered the Red Sea.

29 And the people were between two walls.

30 And they said one unto another: It is better for us to be drowned in the Red Sea than to be slain by the Egyptians.

CHAP XI.

1 *The Israelites pass the Red Sea.* 6 *Pharaoh pursues them to the banks of the Red Sea.* 10 *Miriam and the virgins dance.* 16 *Pharaoh follows them into the Red Sea.* 19 *The sea returns and drowns the Egyptians.* 23 *Moses' song.*

1 AND it came to pass about the seventh hour of that night, in which the children of Israel were encamped on the Red Sea, that Aaron with the people began to pass through the waters.

2 And there went into the Red Sea of the children of Israel, six hundred thousand men on foot, besides women and

A. M. 2513. children: and few fell by the way.

3 And the sun and the moon saw all that was done.

4 And it came to pass on the morrow, that it was told unto Pharaoh, and unto those that were with him, saying:

5 Behold the children of Israel are fled: behold even now they cross the Red Sea.

6 And Pharaoh and his host pursued after them, by the way of Baal-zephon: even to the banks of the Red Sea did they pursue them.

7 And the Egyptians said one to another, We cannot go in after the Hebrews, because of our chariots and our horsemen: for the way is not prepared for them.

8 And moreover should we pass through the sea: peradventure the Israelites shall slay us in the wilderness.

9 And Israel escaped that day out of the hands of the Egyptians: and Israel saw the Egyptians stay on the banks of the sea.

10 ¶ And Miriam said in the presence of Moses, and of Aaron, and of all the elders of Israel:

11 Behold! the waters are as a wall between us, and the Egyptians: so that they cannot come nigh unto us, to destroy us.

12 And Miriam said, Sound the trumpet: bring forth the timbrel, lead up the dance.

13 And Miriam, the sister of Moses, with the virgins her companions, danced before the elders of Israel: and they leaped for joy, and they rejoiced exceedingly. A. M. 2513.

14 [¶ And the Egyptians pursued, and went in after them to the midst of the sea, *even* all Pharaoh's horses, his chariots, and his horsemen.

15 And it came to pass, that in the morning watch the Lord looked unto the host of the Egyptians through the pillar of fire and of the cloud, and troubled the host of the Egyptians,

16 And took off their chariot wheels, that they drave them heavily: so that the Egyptians said, Let us flee from the face of Israel; for the Lord fighteth for them against the Egyptians.

17 ¶And the Lord said unto Moses, Stretch out thy hand over the sea, that the waters may come again upon the Egyptians, upon their chariots, and upon their horsemen.

18 And Moses stretched forth his hand over the sea, and the sea returnd to his strength when the morning appeared; and the Egyptians fled against it; and the Lord overthrew the Egyptians in the midst of the sea.

19 And the waters returned, and covered the chariots, and the horsemen, and all the host of Pharaoh that came into the sea after them; there remained not so much as one of them.

A. M. 2513.

20 But the children of Israel walked upon dry land in the midst of the sea; and the waters were a wall unto them on their right hand, and on their left.

21 Thus the Lord saved Israel that day out of the hand of the Egyptians; and Israel saw the Egyptians dead upon the sea shore.

22 And Israel saw that great work which the Lord did upon the Egyptians: and the people feared the Lord, and believed the Lord, and his servant Moses.

23 ¶ Then sang Moses and the children of Israel this song unto the Lord, and spake, saying, I will sing unto the Lord, for he hath triumphed gloriously: the horse and his rider hath he thrown into the sea.

24 The Lord is my strength and song, and he is become my salvation: he is my God, and I will prepare him an habitation; my father's God, and I will exalt him.

25 The Lord is a man of war: the Lord is his name.

26 Pharaoh's chariots and his host hath he cast into the sea: his chosen captains also are drowned in the Red Sea.

27 The depths have covered them: they sank into the bottom as a stone.

28 Thy right hand, O Lord, is become glorious in power: thy right hand, O Lord, hath dashed in pieces the enemy.

29 And in the greatness of thine excellency thou hast overthrown them that rose up against thee: thou sendest forth thy wrath, which consumed them as stubble.

A. M. 2513.

30 And with the blast of thy nostrils the waters were gathered together, the floods stood upright as an heap, and the depths were congealed in the heart of the sea.

31 The enemy said, I will pursue, I will overtake, I will divide the spoil; my lust shall be satisfied upon them; I will draw my sword, my hand shall destroy them.

32 Thou didst blow with thy wind, the sea covered them: they sank as lead in the mighty waters.

33 Who is like unto thee, O Lord, among the gods? who is like thee, glorious in holiness, fearful in praises, doing wonders.

34 Thou stretchedst out thy right hand, the earth swallowed them.

35 Thou in thy mercy hast led forth the people which thou hast redeemed: thou hast guided them in thy strength unto thy holy habitation.

36 The people shall hear, and be afraid: sorrow shall take hold on the inhabitants of Palestina.

37 Then the dukes of Edom shall be amazed; the mighty men of Moab, trembling, shall take hold upon them; all the

A. M. 2513.

inhabitants of Canaan shall melt away.

38 Fear and dread shall fall upon them; by the greatness of thine arm they shall be as still as a stone; till thy people pass over, O Lord, till the people pass over, which thou hast purchased.

39 Thou shalt bring them in, and plant them in the mountain of thine inheritance, in the place, O Lord, which thou hast made for thee to dwell in; in the Sanctuary, O Lord, which thy hands have established.

40 The Lord shall reign for ever and ever.

41 For the horse of Pharaoh went in with his chariots, and with his horsemen into the sea, and the Lord brought again the waters of the sea upon them; but the children of Israel went on dry land in the midst of the sea.]

CHAP XII.

1 *The Israelites go three days' journey from the Red Sea.* 4 *They faint for want of water.* 8 *Are relieved by the observation of Miriam.* 22 *She excites them to till the ground.* 34 *The place is called Elyma.*

1 AND it came to pass, after the children of Israel had rested for seven days, that Moses said unto the elders:

2 Let us go three days' journey into the wilderness, lest we become an eye-sore unto the Egyptians.

A. M. 2513.

3 And the children of Israel, even all the people, journeyed.

4 And it came to pass on the third day, on the evening thereof, that the people fainted for want of water.

5 And they cried unto Moses, and they said, Give us to drink, lest we die.

6 And Moses was vexed, because of the thirst of the children of Israel.

7 And Moses said unto Miriam, his sister, Lo! what shall I do, lest the people faint for want of water.

8 And Miriam said unto Moses, Go thou with me, and I will shew unto thee a well of water, which lieth eastward of the camp of the children of Israel: a spring which oozeth under the shadow of a tree.

9 And Moses went with his sister; and Aaron, and Jasher went also: and they came unto the tree.

10 And when Moses saw the oozing, he said unto Miriam, What is this to the people of Israel.

11 And Miriam said, Dig: and lo the oozing became as a rivulet.

12 And Moses, Aaron, and Jasher were astonished.

13 Then Miriam said, Follow the stream.

14 And they came unto a place, where there were twelve wells of water.

A. M. 2513.

15 And the people sojourneyed there: and the elders of Israel said unto Miriam,

16 Behold! thou hast refreshed the tribes of Jacob, when they fainted for want of water; thou hast led us into the valley of the palm-trees.

17 Say now unto us, that which shall be pleasing unto thee; and that will we do.

18 And Miriam said, Remember now the words of Pharaoh when he spake unto us, Why covet ye to take with you your flocks, and your cattle, for they cannot be sustained in the wilderness.

19 Nevertheless, O my brethren, unto this day have I sustained the male and the female of every flock, and of every herd, and of every fowl, which I brought out of the land of Goshen.

20 And this day do I deliver them unto the children of Israel, them, and their young ones, that they may increase and multiply, and be food for this people.

21 For behold! the place that we are in is barren, and how long we shall dwell therein is not known unto man.

22 Up then, and let us till the ground: let us cultivate the land, that we perish not.

23 Let us bend the bow, let us slay the wild beasts of the field: peradventure it shall come to pass, that the earth shall bring forth of its increase, and the beasts of the field shall become food for us, and for our children.

24 Then answered the elders of the children of Israel, and said:

25 All that Miriam hath spoken, that will we do.

26 Only how shall be sustained, we, our wives, and our children, until the earth give of its increase.

27 And Miriam said, With the silver and gold ye brought out of Egypt, send and buy of the nations, on this side [a]Jordan, oxen, and cattle, and corn, for you, and your children.

28 Moreover, as I journeyed on to the eastward, lo, I saw trees bearing fruit, and an herb of the field, of which I took, and did eat.

29 ¶ And it came to pass on the morrow, that certain men of Israel arose, and went eastward, and found all things even as Miriam had spoken unto them.

30 And they brought of the fruit thereof, and the people did eat daily, and were satisfied.

31 And they sent chosen men into [b]Rephidim, and they bought oxen and sheep, and corn and oil, and wine.

32 Then arose Caleb, with all those who shot with the bow, and they slew the beasts of the field, even the wild beasts thereof, according as Miriam had commanded them.

A. M. 2513.

[a] *Heb.* the stream.

[b] *Heb.* the valley.

A. M. 2524. 33 And the place thereof was called [c]Elyma, because the people were there refreshed with water, and because Miriam had chosen it for the sojourning of the children of Israel.

[c] *Heb.* invigorated

34 And in process of time the children of Israel spread themselves from Elyma, even to Dopkah, unto the borders of the valley of Rephidim, and unto the land of Nebaioth.

35 And they dug ditches, and they planted trees, and they sowed corn.

36 But they built them no houses; under tents in the open fields did they dwell.

CHAP. XIII.

1 *Moses sends spies into Rephidim.* 4 *Sends Caleb to fight against Rephidim.* 6 *Miriam her proposal to Moses.* 10 *Joshua pushes the Amalekites out of the land.*

1 NOW it came to pass, that
2532. Moses spake unto the
elders of Israel, and he said, Behold, I have sent out spies into Rephidim, to search out the land.

2 And lo [a]Amalek dwelleth there, and the children of Amalek have built them houses in Rephidim; they have gotten also flocks, and much cattle and possessions.

[a] *Or,* the licker.

3 Up, let us drive them out of the land, that we may inherit it: for to drive out, and to take possession of the lands of the Gentiles are we come up A. M. 2532.
out of the land of Egypt, out of the house of bondage.

4 And Moses said unto Caleb, Go thou and [b]Joshua, with the chosen men of the bow, up unto Rephidim, and fight against Amalek.

[b] *Heb.* the deliverer.

5 Behold they are but as a handful of men; Israel shall swallow them up.

6 Then spake Miriam unto Moses, and said, Send messengers unto Amalek, peradventure, when he understandeth the intentions of the children of Israel, he will go quietly out of the land.

7 For it is now upwards of four hundred years since our fathers dwelt in Canaan: these people know us not, neither regard they the claim of us their children,

8 Say therefore unto the inhabitants of Rephidim: I will buy with a price all the flocks, the cattle, the herds, and possessions ye are possessed of.

9 That they may have silver and gold, to buy food and raiment in the lands wherein they shall be strangers.

10 And Moses sent Jasher unto Amalek, saying, Rephidim have I chosen for the habitation of the children of Israel; depart thou from thence, for to-morrow before the sun setteth will I possess it.

11 Only this thing will I do, if it shall come to pass, that you, and your people go

A. M. 2532.

quietly out of the valley: then will I buy with a price all the flocks, the cattle, the herds and possessions ye are possessed of.

12 And Amalek said unto Jasher, What meaneth Moses the stranger! Have I done any wrong unto the descendants of Jacob? Will they take from me that which is my own, the land of the Amalekites?

13 And Jasher returned unto Moses, and unto the elders of Israel: and told them all that Amalek had spoken.

14 And Moses called unto Joshua, and he commanded him, saying: Go out, fight against Amalek, smite them with the edge of the sword.

15 For they have rebelled against us; they have not in the least hearkened unto the words of Jacob.

16 ¶ And Caleb and Joshua, with chosen men of the host of Israel, went up against Rephidim; and they pushed the Amalekites out of that land.

CHAP. XIV.

1 *Jethro brings Zipporah to Moses.* 4 *Who meets Jethro at mount Horeb.* 10 *Jethro advises Moses to appoint judges and rulers over the people, and* 32 *to give them laws and ordinances.*

1 AND it came to pass, when Jethro saw that Moses, his son-in-law, was become a prince unto the Hebrews, that he had brought them up out of the land of Egypt into the wilderness, and that he had driven out the Amalekites, and possessed himself of their city, and all the country of Rephidim: A. M. 2533.

2 That he went out to meet Moses: and there went with him Zipporah and her two children whom Moses had sent back.

3 And Jethro came, and his daughter, and her two children: and they encamped at the foot of mount [a]Horeb. [a] *Heb.* drought.

4 And Moses departed from the wilderness of [b]Zin: to meet his father-in-law at mount Horeb. [b] *Heb.* ebony.

5 And Jethro said unto Moses, Behold I am thy father-in-law: this, my daughter Zipporah, thou knowest is thy wife, and these are thy two children: take them unto thy self, as thou hast covenanted with me.

6 And Moses and Jethro were friends.

7 ¶ And it came to pass, that Moses told Jethro all that he had done in Egypt: that he had led the children of Israel through the Red Sea, and had brought them into the wilderness.

8 And this I say unto you, Behold, lift up your eyes, for the number of the children of Jacob exceed the number of thy people: and their dwell-

A. M. ings are from Elyma, even
2533. until thou comest into the val-
ley of Rephidim.

9 And Jethro said, Thou
hast spoken truly: thy people
are a great people, and their
number are without tale.

10 Now therefore hearken
thou unto the voice of Jethro
thy father: Write thou with
a pen all those things which I
shall now say unto thee.

11 For lo at this time thou
judgeth the people daily:
which thing is too heavy for
thee, thou art not able to per-
form it alone.

12 Set over all Israel, rulers
of thousands, and rulers of
hundreds, and rulers of fifties.

13 And let them judge the
people at all seasons appointed
to their charge: they shall
judge of all the small matters;
the great ones shall the people
bring unto thee.

14 So shall the weight there-
of sit easier on thy shoulders,
and the people shall have thee
and thy office in greater esteem.

15 For it will so fall out,
that all those whom thou shalt
make judges over the people,
will hearken unto all things
which thou shalt speak unto
them.

16 And it shall come to
pass, after thou hast done all
this, that thou shalt teach them
laws and ordinances, that thou
mayest direct them in the way
that thy people should walk,
and in the duties that they
must do.

17 Thou shalt say unto the A. M.
children of Jacob, even before 2533.
the elders thereof:

18 Ye shall set apart every
seventh day, for a day of rest:
ye shall not work therein, nei-
ther thou, nor thy wife, nor thy
son, nor thy daughter, nor thy
man-servant, nor thy maid-ser-
vant, nor thy cattle:

19 For on that day, ye shall
rest from your labour: ye shall
bring offerings of your cattle,
your flocks, and your herds,
and of your fowls.

20 And the priests shall slay
them before the congregation:
and the flesh thereof shall ye
roast with fire, and the people
shall eat thereof.

21 And on that day shall the
priests rehearse in the ears of
all Israel, all the wonders which
ye have received from your
forefathers: the mighty things
which thou hast done in the
land of Egypt: and all those
laws and ordinances, thou shalt
appoint unto this people to ob-
serve.

22 Thou shalt say unto the
children of Israel:

23 Ye shall not use Tera-
phim, neither shall ye worship
any one of the gods of the na-
tions: the Lord, the maker of
heaven and earth, shall ye only
worship.

24 Ye shall not speak evil
of the maker of all things.

25 Ye shall reverence the
hoary head.

26 Ye shall not smite any

A. M. 2533. one man so that he die: he that does, shall die the death, and his name shall be forgotten.

27 Ye shall not evil speak of, nor slander any one of the children of Jacob.

28 Ye shall not covet that which appertaineth unto another.

29 Ye shall not do after the abominations of the Egyptians: your sons shall not uncover the nakedness of your daughters.

30 Ye shall not uncover the nakedness of a woman during her uncleanness.

31 Ye shall not uncover the nakedness of the virgin betrothed: neither shalt thou go in unto a woman who is the wife of another.

32 ¶ And Jethro said unto Moses: Moreover, thou shalt teach the children of Israel such other statutes and ordinances, which thou, and the judges thou shalt appoint, shall find needful.

33 And Jethro returned into Midian: and Moses departed for the valley of Rephidim:

CHAP. XV.

1 *Moses attempts to appoint judges;* 4 *is opposed by Miriam.* 7 *He is angry with her.* 8 *Miriam is imprisoned;* 9 *on which the people rise and demand her.* 11 *She is set at liberty, and the people rejoice.* 15 *Miriam dies, and the people mourn.* 16 *Her character.*

2534. 1 AND it came to pass, that Moses assembled the elders and all the children of Israel together, nigh unto mount [a] Sinai. A. M. 2534.

2 And Moses said unto the people: Choose ye out from among you, seventy men, according to your tribes, that they may judge for you.

3 That there may be rulers of thousands, rulers of hundreds, and rulers of fifties.

4 And Miriam arose and said, Shall Jethro instruct the Hebrews? Are the children of Jacob without understanding?

5 Are the customs of the Midianites to be brought in among us? Are we to forsake the good old paths in which our fathers, even Abraham, Isaac, and Jacob, have trod.

6 And the voice of the tribes of the congregation were on the side of Miriam.

7 And the anger of Moses was greatly kindled against Miriam: and Moses sought to cut Miriam off from the congregation.

8 And Moses hid Miriam for seven days; and the congregation wotted not what was come unto her.

9 And the people of Israel gathered themselves together unto Moses, and said:

10 Bring forth unto us Miriam, our counsellor, for according to all she hath spoken we will do.

11 Then Moses brought forth Miriam, and presented her before the congregation.

[a] *Heb.* watchful.

A. M. 2534. 12 And when the people saw Miriam that she was well, they rejoiced greatly, with exceeding great joy.

13 And all the days of Miriam, the children of Israel did according to all the words of Abraham, of Isaac, and of Jacob.

14 ¶ And Miriam went and dwelt in Kadesh.

2539. 15 And Miriam died there. And the children of Israel mourned for Miriam forty days: neither did any man go forth of his dwelling.

16 ¶ And the lamentation was great; for after Miriam arose up no one like unto her of the daughters of Jacob: no, not even unto this day.

17 And the fame thereof went out into all the lands of the Gentiles; yea, throughout all Canaan. And the nations feared greatly.

CHAP. XVI.

2 *Moses takes Jethro's advice.* 5 *He builds an altar.* 6 *Twelve young men chosen;* 7 *who slay the offerings.* 11 *Seventy elders chosen.* 13 *Moses and the seventy elders go up mount Sinai.*

2540. 1 AND it came to pass after the lamentation for Miriam was over, that Jethro came unto mount Sinai, and he spake unto Moses, saying:

2 Thus saith Jethro, the priest of Midian, Thou shalt appoint rulers of the people, according to all that which I
have spoken unto you at the A. M. 2540.
foot of Horeb.

3 And Moses hearkened unto the words of Jethro, his father-in-law: and he obeyed his voice in all that he had commanded him.

4 ¶ And Moses said unto [a]Nadab and [b]Abihu, the sons of Aaron: Go to now, and build ye an altar, even as Jethro hath dictated unto you.

[a] *Heb.* popular.
[b] *Heb.* willed

5 And Nadab and Abihu builded an altar nigh unto mount Sinai, even as Jethro had dictated: and they set up twelve pillars, according to the number of the tribes of the children of Israel.

6 And Moses chose out from among the congregation, twelve young men; men of strength and renown.

7 And Moses commanded them, saying: Behold the people have brought oxen and sheep for a peace-offering, slay them before the altar, and roast the flesh thereof with fire, that the people may eat of the fat thereof, and be satisfied.

8 And the young men, the priests, did so: and the congregation did eat before Sinai, and the people were well pleased.

9 And Moses stood forth and said, The work is great, and the number of the children of Israel, the Lord, the God of our fathers, hath multiplied exceedingly: and he

A. M. 2540.

will increase them daily, even until their number shall be as the stars of the firmament.

10 It is meet therefore that ye choose out from among you, seventy elders, that they may assist me, and Aaron, and Joshua, and Nadab, and Abihu, the servants of the Lord.

11 And the congregation did as Moses had spoken.

12 ¶ And in those days it came to pass, that Moses spake unto Aaron, and unto [c] Hur, saying:

[c] *Heb.* clothed in white.

13 Stay ye with the people here, and judge them, for lo, I shall go up on the mount with Joshua, Nadab, and Abihu, and the elders; and we shall stay there forty days and forty nights.

14 ¶ And I, Jasher, the son of Caleb, bare the rod before Moses and Joshua, and the seventy elders of the people.

CHAP. XVII.

1 *Jethro meets Moses on mount Sinai.* 5 *Jethro's counsel, concerning building the tabernacle.* 9 *Institution of the priesthood.* 10 *Aaron's family is chosen.* 11 *Holy vestments appointed.* 12 *The ark.* 14 *The people murmur.* 21 *Moses, his proposal.* 22 *Nadab and Abihu only dissent.* 24 *Moses descends from the mount.* 28 *The tribe of Levi made holy.*

1 NOW it came to pass on the morrow, that Jethro met Moses, Joshua, Nadab, Abihu, and the seventy elders, on the mount; and the trumpet sounded.

A. M. 2543.

2 And Jethro said unto Moses, Thou hast done well: in that thou hast chosen out wise men to be counsellors unto thee.

3 And Jethro bowed himself before Moses, Joshua, Nadab, and Abihu, and before the seventy elders.

4 ¶ And on the second day, about the ninth hour thereof, the trumpet sounded, and Jethro, Moses' father-in-law, stood forth and said:

5 Behold, thus saith Jethro, the son of [a] Esau, the priest of Midian: It is meet, O Israel! that ye build a tabernacle for the God, the maker of heaven and of earth; even for the God of Abraham, the God of Isaac, and the God of Jacob, that ye may serve the Lord, who hath delivered ye out of the hands of the Egyptians, and from the dangers of the Red Sea.

[a] *Heb.* the hairy

6 Then Moses, Joshua, Nadab, and Abihu, and the seventy elders, answered Jethro, and said:

7 The Lord, our God, hath been merciful unto us: and the light of his countenance hath shone upon us.

8 Then Jethro instructed Moses in what manner, and in what form, and with what materials he should build the tabernacle of the Lord of Hosts.

A. M. 2543.

9 And thus saith Jethro: When ye have builded the tabernacle, ye shall appoint priests to minister before the Lord: according to the tribes of the children of Israel, shall ye appoint.

10 And Moses, Joshua, Nadab, and Abihu, and the seventy elders, said: Let Aaron and his sons be set apart as sanctified unto the Lord.

11 Then said Jethro unto Moses, Thou shalt put upon Aaron and his sons, the garments which thou hast seen, that they may be a holy priesthood unto the Lord, the God of Israel.

12 Moreover, ye shall build an ark unto the Lord, wherein ye shall lay up before the Lord the testimony; even the writings of the laws and ordinances which ye shall receive.

13 And it came to pass, when the forty days were fulfilled, wherein Jethro communed with Moses, Joshua, and the seventy elders, that all the statutes and the ordinances to be observed, were written in a book of remembrance.

14 ¶ And it came to pass, whilst Moses, Joshua, Nadab, and Abihu, and the seventy elders, tarried in the mount, that the people murmured, and they said one among another,

15 Whether is it better, that we be the subjects of the Egyptians whom we know: Up, let us return thither, we, our wives, and our children: or become the slaves, and walk after the laws and customs of Jethro, the Midianite, whom we know not?

A. M. 2543.

16 And the people spake unto Aaron, saying: Moses, who, by his cunning, hath brought us up out of the land of Egypt, now seeketh to make himself a king and a ruler over us.

17 And Aaron answered the people, and he said: On the morning of the third day, ye shall assemble according to your tribes, and I will do all that which ye shall then speak unto me.

18 ¶ Then Aaron sent messengers unto Moses, Joshua, Nadab, and Abihu, and the seventy elders, on the mount, and they spake before them, saying:

19 Thus saith Aaron, thy brother, because ye tarry on the mount, the people murmur, and say, Whether is it better, that we be the subjects of the Egyptians whom we know: Up, let us return thither, we, our wives, and our children; or become the slaves, and walk after the laws and customs of Jethro, the Midianite, whom we know not?

20 And when Moses had heard these things he was exceeding wroth.

21 ¶ Then Moses, after he had sent away the messengers,

A. M. 2543. spake unto Joshua, Nadab, and Abihu, and the seventy elders:

22 Behold, thus it behoveth us to say unto the people: We have seen the Lord in the mount, we have ate and drank in his presence, and the words which he hath spoken unto us, they are those which we now deliver unto you.

23 And the saying of Moses was pleasing unto Joshua, and unto the seventy elders: but unto Nadab and Abihu it was not pleasing.

24 And Nadab and Abihu were cut off from the assembly: and they hastened into the camp of the children of Israel, which lay at the foot of mount Sinai.

25 ¶ And it came to pass on the fortieth morning after Moses, Joshua, and the seventy elders had gone up on the mount, that the trumpet sounded: and Moses, Joshua, and the seventy elders, assayed to come down from the mount.

26 And as they descended, Joshua spake unto Moses, and said, Lo, Nadab and Abihu have joined themselves unto the people: and the voice of the people seemeth as the voice of rebellion.

27 And it was told unto Moses, and unto Joshua, saying, The voice of the people is the voice of shouting, and of great joy: lo, Aaron, Hur, Nadab, and Abihu stand up before the people. A. M. 2543.

28 ¶ Then Moses called for Aaron, and he said unto him, The Lord hath chosen thee, and thy sons, to minister before the Lord, in the tabernacle which ye shall build.

29 Separate therefore yourselves, thou, and thy sons, even all the tribe of Levi, that ye may be a holy priesthood unto the Lord.

30 And Moses came down from the mount: he, and Joshua, and the seventy elders of the people.

CHAP. XVIII.

3 Nadab and Abihu rebel. 6 The Levites slay three thousand of the people. 8 The people repent. 12 They build a tabernacle, 18 and an altar. 19 Aaron and his sons are to be clothed.

1 AND it came to pass on the morrow, that Moses stood before the people, at the entrance into the camp, and he said:

2 Who is on the Lord's side? Let him come forth of the camp.

3 And Aaron, and all the sons of the tribe of Levi, except Nadab and Abihu, came forth of the camp, and stood before Moses.

4 And Joshua said unto Moses: Lo, the people have spoken well of Nadab and Abihu; and they have eaten, and they have drank, and be-

A. M. 2543.

hold, now they are risen up to play.

5 ¶ Then said Moses unto the sons of Levi, even unto all the tribe thereof: Gird on each man his sword, and go ye through the camp, and slay ye the froward, even every man his friend.

6 And they did so: and they slew Nadab and Abihu, the sons of Aaron, with three thousand of the people.

7 But Aaron held his peace.

8 ¶ And it came to pass, when the slaughter was over, that the children of Israel humbled themselves, and they said:

9 All that the [a] Lord shall say unto us, that will we do.

10 And the people sent messengers unto Moses, and unto Aaron, and unto Joshua, and unto the seventy elders, saying:

11 We have done wrong; we have sinned; intreat ye for us.

12 And Moses said, Thus saith the Lord, Ye shall build a tabernacle unto my name, wherein my honour shall dwell.

13 [b] Bezaliel and [c] Aholiab are endued with understanding, in all manner of workmanship, in cunning works, in works of gold, and in works of silver: lo, they shall build the tabernacle according to all that I shall say unto them.

14 And Bezaliel and Aholiab built the tabernacle for the congregation; with the offerings of the children of Israel, even of gold, of silver, of brass, and of fine linen.

15 ¶ This is my sanctuary: and I will dwell among my people from this day forth, for evermore.

16 ¶ And it came to pass, that Moses went into the tabernacle, in the sight of all the children of Israel.

17 And Moses came forth to the door of the tabernacle, and spake before the congregation, and said:

18 Thus saith the Lord, Ye shall build an altar before the door of the tabernacle: and ye shall offer thereon burnt-offerings, and lambs, and kids of a year old: and Aaron and his sons shall minister before me.

19 ¶ And thus shalt thou clothe Aaron: Thou shalt put upon Aaron, the coat, the ephod, the breast-plate, the mitre, and the crown.

20 And on his sons, even on all the males of the tribe of Levi, who are able to stand before the congregation, ye shall put on coats, girdles, and bonnets.

21 Thus shall ye consecrate Aaron and his sons: and they shall minister before me for ever.

A. M. 2543.

[a] *Or,* ruler.

[b] *Heb.* according to the pattern of the Lord.

[c] *Heb.* the builder.

A. M.
2544.

CHAP. XIX.

1 *Moses reads the law before the congregation.* 17 *They promise to observe the ordinances and statutes.*

1 AND it came to pass on
the morrow, that Mo-
ses read before the congrega-
tion, out of the book of the
covenant, the statutes and
ordinances which the Lord
had appointed unto the children
of Israel to observe.
2 And Moses said, Thus
saith the Lord, the God of
Abraham, the God of Isaac,
and the God of Jacob: I am
the Lord, thy God, with my
outstretched arm have I deli-
vered ye from the bondage of
the Egyptians; ye shall wor-
ship no other god beside me.
3 The likeness of the Lord,
thy God, thou shalt not make,
either in gold, in silver, in
brass, or in wood: thou shalt
not use Teraphim in thy dwel-
lings, saith the Lord.
4 Sacred and holy shall my
name be, in the mouths of this
congregation: and in the
mouths of your sons, and your
sons' sons, throughout all ge-
nerations.
5 Ye shall set apart every
seventh day, for a day of rest:
thou shalt not work therein,
neither thou, thy wife, nor
thy son, nor thy daughter, nor
thy man-servant, nor thy maid-
servant, nor thy cattle, nor the
stranger that shall be within A. M.
thy gate. 2544.
6 For on that day, thou
shalt rest from thy labour:
and on that day thou shalt
bring offerings of thy cattle,
of thy flocks, of thy herds,
and of thy fowls.
7 And the priests shall slay
them before the congregation:
and the flesh thereof shall they
roast with fire.
8 And on that day shall the
priest rehearse in the ears of all
Israel, all the wonders done in
the land of Egypt, and in the
Red Sea.
9 Thou shalt reverence the
hoary head.
10 Thou shalt not smite
any man, so that he die: if
thou dost, thou shalt die the
death, and thy name shall be
forgotten.
11 Thou shalt not speak
evil of, nor slander any of the
children of Jacob.
12 Thou shalt not covet
that which is the property
of another.
13 Thou shalt not do after
the abominations of the Egyp-
tians: thou shalt not uncover
the nakedness of thy sister, she
is thy own flesh.
14 Thou shalt not uncover
the nakedness of a woman
during her uncleanness.
15 Thou shalt not uncover
the nakedness of the virgin be-
trothed: neither shalt thou go
in unto a woman who is the
wife of another.

A. M. 2544. 16 ¶ And when Moses had made an end of speaking, all the people cried out with one voice:

17 All these things which the Lord hath commanded, will we observe to do: we, and our sons, and our sons' sons, for ever.

CHAP XX.

2 The ark is built. 5 The mercy-seat. 6 The table. 7 The vessels. 8 The incense-altar. 11 The hangings. 16 Priests to be without blemish.

2545. 1 AND Moses said, Behold, thus saith the Lord, Ye shall build an ark unto the Lord, and he shall put the ark into the tabernacle of the congregation: and he shall lay up therein the words of the testimony, which I have read this day in the ears of all Israel, for a perpetual memorial of the covenant which the Lord hath made with the posterity of Jacob.

2 ¶ And Bezaliel and Aholiab made the ark according to the pattern they had received of the Lord, on mount Sinai.

3 And the ark was of Shittim-wood: two cubits and a half was the length of it, and a cubit and a half the breadth of it, and the height a cubit and a half.

4 And they made four rings of gold, two on each side, and they made two staves also: that the priests might bear the ark of the testimony before the people. A. M. 2545.

5 Then made they the mercy-seat of pure gold, and the cherubims at each corner thereof: of pure gold did they make them.

6 The table of Shittim-wood made they, and they overlaid it with gold: and they cast four rings of gold, and they made staves to bear the table.

7 And the vessels of the table, the dishes, the spoons, the bowls, the covers, the candlesticks, the six branches thereof; and the seven lamps, the snuffers, and snuff-dishes, of beaten gold were they made.

8 The incense-altar of Shittim-wood was four-square, and the horns thereof of the same, overlaid with pure gold, with rings and with staves to bear it withal.

9 Of Shittim-wood also did they make the altar of the burnt-offering, and the horns thereof, and the staves thereof: and with brass did they overlay it.

10 The pots, the shovels, the basons, the fire-pans, the grates, the four rings, the laver, the twenty pillars with their sockets: all of brass did they make them.

11 And of fine linen were made the hangings of the tabernacle, and the hangings of the gate of the court were of

A. M. 2545.

blue, of scarlet, and of purple, wrought in needle-work, by the virgins of Israel: according to the pattern Moses had received of the Lord, on the mount.

12 For they brought unto Moses, day by day, all the work which they had done: and Moses looked on the same, that it might be done according to all that the Lord had commanded him.

13 ¶ And Moses said, Thus hath the Lord spoken, Thou shalt put the ark of the covenant, the table, the mercy-seat, with all the furniture thereof, into the tabernacle of the congregation.

14 Before the door of the tabernacle shalt thou build the altar, with the laver, and with the hangings thereof: and with oil shalt thou sanctify them.

15 Aaron, and his sons, shalt thou bring before the door of the tabernacle of the congregation: and thou shalt wash them with water, and thou shalt anoint them with oil.

16 Only this thing shalt thou observe, All the males of the tribe of Levi, without blemish, shalt thou consecrate, saith the Lord: the eunuch, whether he be born so, or made so, shalt thou not consecrate.

17 And the burnt-offerings, and the sacrifices, and the offerings of kids, and of goats, and of sheep, and of oxen, and of purple, and of scarlet, and of fine linen, which the people offered, appertained unto the Levites, even as the Lord had commanded Moses.

A. M. 2545.

18 ¶ Thus did Moses in the sight of all Israel: even according to the commandment of the Lord, did he.

CHAP. XXI.

1 *Korah, his rebellion.* 11 *He and his company destroyed by fire.* 13 *The people fear greatly.* 15 *The priesthood established.*

1 AND when Korah, [a] Dathan, [b] Abiram, and [c] On, with two hundred and fifty of the children of Israel, men famous in the congregation, and men of renown, saw all that was done,

[a] *Heb.* the rites.
[b] *Heb.* the father of deceit.
[c] *Heb.* iniquity.

2 They said one to the other: This thing which Moses and Aaron have done, is not of the Lord.

3 For behold, henceforward shall the tribe of Levi live on the fat of the land, they shall be clothed in soft raiment; they shall fare sumptuously every day; the plough and the axe shall they be strangers to: and lo! we, and our sons, and our sons' sons, shall they gall with the yoke that this day they have brought upon us.

4 And they gathered themselves together unto Moses, and they said unto him:

5 What thing is this that thou hast done? Are not all

A. M. 2545. the people holy? Wherefore hast thou separated the tribe of Levi, to be sanctified unto the Lord?

6 Hast thou not brought us into the wilderness? Should not all help to till the ground? yea, the hands of the people are not equal to the task: and shalt thou take away every tenth man from the labour.

7 And Moses said, To-morrow shall the Lord answer the blasphemies you now utter: and shew who is holy, and who is not holy.

8 ¶ And it came to pass on the morrow, that Korah, Dathan, and Abiram, with the two hundred and fifty men of the children of Israel, assembled themselves together before the door of the tabernacle of the congregation.

9 And Moses spake unto them, and said, Behold, O Korah, Dathan, and Abiram, thus saith the Lord, Ye fight against me, even against the God of your fathers, the God of Abraham, the God of Isaac, and the God of Jacob, who hath brought you up out of the land of Egypt, out of the house of bondage.

10 And Moses said unto the congregation: Separate yourselves from Korah and his company, peradventure the Lord will do a new thing.

11 And they did so: and Korah and his company stood before the tabernacle.

12 And Moses commanded the Levites, saying: Up now, slay Korah, Dathan, and Abiram, with those that are with them, with fire, even as the Lord hath spoken unto me. A. M. 2545.

13 And Korah, Dathan, and Abiram, with the two hundred and fifty men of the children of Israel, perished by fire before the door of the tabernacle of the Lord.

14 And great fear fell on all the congregation: and they hastened every man to his tent.

15 ¶ Thus did Moses establish the priesthood in his brother's house, in the tribe of Levi: and he committed unto them, the keeping of the tabernacle, of the ark, and of the book of the testimony, according to all that the Lord had commanded him.

CHAP. XXII.

1 *Israel enjoys peace.* 4 *They defile themselves with the women of Midian and Moab.*

1 AFTER these days it came 2546.
to pass, that the people obeyed the voice of the Lord, by the mouth of his servant Moses.

2 And there was peace throughout all the tribes of the children of Israel.

3 For no man opened his mouth against Zipporah: nor against the women of Midian, her companions, nor against those of Moab.

A. M. 2546. 4 ¶ And in process of time, the women of Midian, and the women of Moab, became conversant with the sons of Israel.

5 During all the days of Jethro, Moses' father-in-law, and all the days of Zipporah, Moses' wife.

6 And the children of Israel defiled themselves with the women of Midian, and with the women of Moab: and they learned to walk after all their abominations.

CHAP. XXIII.

2 *Aaron reads out of the book of the covenant divers laws concerning trespasses, and their atonements.* 18 *The passover and feasts instituted;* 23 *Shelomite, his blasphemy.* 26 *He is stoned.*

2547. 1 AND it came to pass after many days, that Moses assembled the congregation of the children of Israel together; even all the tribes thereof, to the door of the tabernacle of the Lord.

2 And he brought forth the book of the covenant, and Aaron read it before the congregation, in the sight of all Israel.

3 And Aaron said, Thus saith the Lord, by his servant Moses: If any man bring an offering unto the Lord, he shall bring it voluntarily; it shall be a male without blemish, of his flock, of his cattle, and of the prime of his fowl.

4 He shall bring the male of his flock unto the priests, the sons of Aaron: and they shall slay it before the door of the tabernacle, and they shall cut it in pieces, and they shall lay it on the altar on the fire which they shall make; and they shall roast the flesh thereof, which is acceptable, and a sweet savour, as the Lord hath appointed. A. M. 2547.

5 And when any man shall bring a meal-offering unto the Lord, he shall offer of fine flour, unleavened, mixed with oil and frankincense; and the priests shall bake it on the altar, and they shall eat thereof; it is a thing done by fire, and is of a sweet savour.

6 And thou shalt bring an oblation of thy first fruits unto the Lord; and with all thy offerings, thou shalt offer salt.

7 The peace-offering, whether it be of the herd, of the flock, or of the field, it shall be the best; without blemish shalt thou bring it before the Lord.

8 If thou dost sin through ignorance, against any of the commandments of the Lord, thou shalt bring before the door of the tabernacle of the congregation, a young bullock, or a kid, or a lamb, without blemish; and the priest shall kill the bullock, or the kid, or the lamb, and he shall roast them with fire, on the altar, without the gate of the camp,

A. M. 2547.

and thy sin shall be forgiven thee.

9 If thou shalt touch any unclean thing, whether it be of man, or of beast, thou shalt bring unto the priest, a lamb, or a kid of thy goats, or two turtle doves, or an ephah of fine flour: and he shall make an atonement for thee.

10 If thou shalt commit a trespass unwittingly, then shalt thou bring a ram, without blemish, with the estimation thereof, in shekels of silver; and when thou hast satisfied the trespass, thou shalt add the fifth part thereof, and thou shalt give it unto the priest, who shall make an atonement for thee, and thy trespass shall be forgiven.

11 If thou shalt trespass, wittingly, against thy neighbour, by taking that which is his, thou shalt restore it to the full estimation thereof; and thou shalt give him a fifth part more: and then thou shalt bring unto the priest, a ram, without blemish, with its value in shekels of silver; and the priest shall make an atonement for thee, and thou shalt be forgiven.

12 And the priests, the sons of Aaron, shall eat of the sin-offering, of the peace-offering, and of the trespass-offering; according to all which the Lord commanded Moses in mount Sinai.

13 ¶ Thus saith the Lord, Aaron, or his sons, shall not drink wine nor strong drink, when they are to minister before the congregation, that they may discern between the clean and the unclean; and that they may teach the children of Israel my statutes.

A. M. 2547.

14 Thus saith the Lord, When a woman hath borne a child, whether it be a male-child, or a maid-child, she shall be unclean thirty and three days; and she shall bring a lamb of the first year, or two turtle doves, or two young pigeons, and she shall bring them unto the priest, and he shall make an atonement for her, and she shall be clean.

15 ¶ Thus saith the Lord, When a man shall have in his flesh the plague of the leprosy, he shall be brought unto Aaron, or unto one of his sons, who shall look on him, and if he be unclean, he shall put him out of the camp, until he shall be healed of his sore; and then he shall bring unto the priest, two he-lambs, without blemish, and three tenth-deals of fine flour, mingled with oil, with one log of oil, and the priest shall wave them before the Lord, and shall make an atonement for him, and he shall be clean.

16 Thus saith the Lord, Whilst a woman is unclean in her flesh, she shall be put apart seven days, no man shall approach unto her during her

A. M. uncleanness; and when she is
2547. cleansed of her issue, she shall
take two turtle doves, or two
young pigeons, and bring them
unto the priest, to the door of
the tabernacle; and he shall
make an atonement for her,
and she shall be clean.
17 ¶ And it shall come to
pass, on the seventh month, in
every year, when the congre-
gation of the children of Israel
hath sinned against the Lord,
that every man shall bring an
offering according to his esti-
mation; and the priests shall
wave every man's oblation be-
fore the Lord, at the door of
the tabernacle of the congre-
gation, and the priests shall
make atonement for the sins
of all the people of Israel, and
they shall be forgiven their
sins, which they have sinned
against the Lord.
18 ¶ Moreover thus shall
ye do, on the fourteenth day
of the first month: at even
shall be the feast of the pass-
over unto the Lord.
19 And the next day shall
be the feast of unleavened
bread unto the Lord, for seven
days.
20 And on the tenth, there
shall be a day of atonement;
wherein ye shall afflict your
souls.
21 And on the fifteenth day
shall be the feast of taberna-
cles; with boughs, and with
branches of palm-trees, and
with willows of the brook,
shall ye rejoice before the Lord, A. M.
for seven days. 2547.
22 Thus did Moses esta-
blish the feasts of the Lord;
even as he was commanded on
mount Sinai.
23 ¶ Then came forth the
son of Shelomith before the
congregation, and spake unto
Moses, at the door of the ta-
bernacle, saying:
24 The Lord hath not
spoken these things; perad-
venture they are imaginations
of evil to this people.
25 And Moses commanded
the Levites, saying, Lead him
forth of the camp, and let
the people stone him with
stones, that he die, as the Lord
hath spoken.
26 And they did so: and
the people stoned him to
death; because he had blas-
phemed before Moses, and
because he had spoken evil in
Israel.

CHAP. XXIV.

1 *Twelve spies sent into Canaan.* 10 *Ten bring an evil report.* 11 *Caleb and Joshua encourage the people.* 18 *The ten are stoned.* 20 *Jethro dies.* 22 *Zipporah dies.* 23 *Aaron dies.*

1 AND it came to pass, 2548.
when the days of the
sojourning of the children
of Israel in the wilderness
were multiplied, that Moses
spake unto the elders, and
unto all the congregation of
Israel, saying:

A. M. 2548.

2 Thus saith the Lord, Send chosen men to search out the land of Canaan, according to the number of the tribes, twelve men: men of wisdom, that ye may go in, and possess the land which I have given unto you.

3 And the men who were sent, were [a] Shammua, [b] Shaphat, Caleb, [c] Igal, Joshua, [d] Palti, [e] Gaddiel, [f] Gaddi, [g] Ammiel, [h] Sethur, [i] Nahbi, and [k] Geuel.

[a] *Heb.* obeying.
[b] *Heb.* the judicious.
[c] *Heb.* the redeemed.
[d] *Heb.* freed.
[e] *Heb.* the expeditious.
[f] *Heb.* girded.
[g] *Heb.* God with me.
[h] *Heb.* exploring
[i] *Heb.* the reserved.
[k] *Heb.* the celebrated.

4 These are the names of the men whom Moses sent into Canaan, to spy out the land.

5 And Moses said unto them, Go into Canaan this way, and go up on yonder mountain; and from thence, see the land, and bring unto me, and the congregation of Israel, word, whether the people therein be strong or weak, or few or many.

6 Whether the land be a land flowing with milk and with honey: and what cities they have builded, their strong holds, their tents, and their houses, shall you note.

7 ¶ Then went forth the spies, and they did as Moses had commanded: and they brought with them of the fruit of the land, and they returned in forty days.

8 And the men who were sent, spake unto Moses, and Aaron, and unto the congregation, saying:

A. M. 2548.

9 Surely the land of Canaan, whether ye sent us, is a land flowing with milk and with honey: and behold, this is the fruit thereof.

10 But as for the people, they be strong, and their cities be walled, and exceeding great: [l] Anak, and his sons, dwell there, with our enemies, the Amalekites, the Hittites, the Jebusites, and the Amorites.

[l] *Heb.* huge.

11 And Caleb, even he who taught Israel to shoot with the bow, stood forth and said, Up, let us gird on the sword, and take the bow, peradventure we shall possess the land, for we are more mighty than the people of the nations; and the Lord is with us, and he will prosper us.

12 And Joshua said, Caleb hath spoken the truth.

13 Then said the other men who were sent with Caleb and Joshua unto Moses, and unto all the congregation, ten were they in number, We cannot stand before this people, for they are stronger, and in stature we appear unto them as dwarfs; the sons of Anak are giants: lo! we shall never be able to go in and possess the land.

14 And they sowed sedition among the people: and the children of Israel murmured, and said:

15 Wherefore hath Moses and Aaron brought us hither, that we, our wives, and our

A. M. 2548.

children, fall by the sword of the Gentiles.

16 And they said as one man: Shammua shall be our captain, and we will return into the land of Egypt.

17 ¶ Then spake Caleb, the son of [m]Jephunneh, and Joshua, the son of [n]Nun, These men, who went with us, have brought an evil report on the land: for the land is good, it floweth with milk and with honey: and the Lord, the God of our fathers, hath delivered the people thereof into our hand.

[m] *Heb.* regarding.
[n] *Heb.* the steady

18 And Moses said, They have blasphemed; they have lied unto the Lord: and the Levites, and the congregation, stoned them with stones, before the door of the tabernacle.

19 Then dwelt Israel in peace, and listened unto the words of the Lord, which he spake by the mouth of Moses, his servant.

2550. 20 ¶ And it was told unto Moses, that Jethro, his father-in-law, was dead.

21 And [o]Balak, the king of Moab, was king of Midian: now Balak was not the son of Jethro.

[o] *Heb.* pulled down.

22 And Zipporah, Jethro's daughter, the wife of Moses, died also: but the children of Israel mourned not.

23 And Aaron went up into mount [p]Hor, and died there, and was buried.

[p] *Heb.* steep.

CHAP. XXV.

A. M. 2551.

1 Moses exhorteth the people to go into Canaan. 6 Balak opposeth the designs of Moses. 14 The Midianites, the Moabites, and the Amorites, are smitten, except the women; 18 with whom the Israelites defile themselves. 23 The Levites hang up the chiefs. 26 The women of Midian are slain, save the virgins. 30 Moses divideth the spoil. 40 The Reubenites desire to have their inheritance on this side Jordan. 47 It is granted on condition.

1 AND the trumpet sounded before Moses, and before [a]Eleazer, the priest, and before the elders, at the door of the tabernacle: and all Israel assembled to hear the words of the Lord.

[a] *Heb.* the porch of the Lord.

2 And Moses said, The days of the accomplishment of the promise, which the Lord hath made unto our fathers, that their seed shall inherit the land of Canaan, is at hand.

3 Arm therefore to the war, so many of you, according to your tribes: one thousand out of every tribe, shall ye number.

4 And Joshua, and Caleb, and [b]Phinehas, the priest, with the holy trumpets, shall go before you, and lead you into the land whereof the Lord hath said: Thy seed shall possess the land of Canaan, as I sware unto thy fathers; a land flowing with milk and honey.

[b] *Heb.* confiding

A. M. 2551.

5 The Amorites, the Moabites, the Midianites, the Jebusites, and all the nations of Canaan: they shall not stand before you, saith the Lord.

6 ¶ Now it came to pass, that when Balak, the king of [c]Moab, had heard all that had been spoken by Moses, that he assembled the princes of Moab and of Midian, with those of the Amorites, and he said unto them:

[c] *Heb.* incest.

7 Behold! Moses, with the Hebrews who have followed him out of Egypt, draw nigh unto our land to dispossess us, and to drive us out from the heritage of our fathers.

8 Now therefore send messengers unto [d]Balaam, the king of [e]Mesopotamia, lest when they have destroyed us, they destroy him, and his people also.

[d] *Heb.* grave.

[e] *Or,* Mediterranean.

9 And the messengers came unto Pethor, and spake unto Balaam: Lo! the Hebrews, who are come up out of Egypt, have set their faces against us, join thou with us, that neither we, nor thy servants, be slain.

10 Then Balaam assembled the princes of Mesopotamia together, and he said unto them: Lo! Balak, king of Moab and of Midian, hath sent unto us, that we fight with them against Moses and the Hebrews, who have now set their faces against the Midianites, the Moabites, and the Amorites, to dispossess and destroy them.

11 And the princes said, Why should we fight against Israel, seeing we dwell in the land between the two rivers? A. M. 2551.

12 And the messengers returned unto Balak: and Balak was disheartened.

13 ¶ Then went forth Joshua, Caleb, and Phinehas, the priest, with the holy instruments, and with the trumpets, and it was proclaimed, saying:

14 Smite the Midianites, even all the males thereof: but the females ye shall not touch.

15 And they did so: and there fell that day all the males of the children of Midian, of Moab, and of the nations.

16 Then returned Phinehas, Joshua, and Caleb, with all Israel, that went forth to the battle.

17 And they brought into the camp of Israel, all the wives of the Midianites, of the Moabites, and of the Amorites, with the virgins: even all the females.

18 And the elders, and all the children of Israel, defiled themselves with the women of Midian, with the women of Moab, and with the women of the nations.

19 And children of the women of Midian, Moab, and the nations, were born unto the elders of the people of Israel.

20 And the people did evil in the sight of the Lord.

A. M. 2551. 21 ¶ Then Moses, with Eleazar, the priest, stood forth and said:

22 Ye have sinned, in that ye have saved the women of the nations when ye fought against them; and the Lord delivered the people into your hands.

23 And Moses spake unto the Levites, and said, Thus saith the Lord: Take the heads of those who have sinned, and hang them up before the door of the tabernacle of the Lord, in the sight of all the congregation.

24 And they hung them up in the sun, in the sight of all Israel.

25 And there fell of the people, twenty and four thousand, and then the slaughter ceased.

2552. 26 Then Moses spake unto the children of Israel, and said, Thus saith the Lord: ye shall slay all the women of the nations with whom ye have defiled yourselves, and the males born unto them; you shall save for yourselves only the virgin who hath not lain with man.

27 And the children of Israel did according to all that they were commanded.

28 And the number of the women-children, virgins, were thirty and two thousand, who knew not man.

29 ¶ And it came to pass, after these things, that Moses said, Bring forth the spoil of the Moabites, the Midianites, and of the nations. A. M. 2552.

30 For thus saith the Lord, The prey shall ye divide; the one half thereof shall be for those who took the war upon them, and the other half shall ye give unto the congregation of the Lord.

31 Now the half that pertained unto the men, even unto those of each tribe who came from the war, were of sheep, three hundred and seven and thirty thousand and five hundred: of beeves, thirty and six thousand: of asses, thirty thousand and five hundred: and of virgins, sixteen thousand.

32 But of these, the tribute unto the Lord, were of the sheep, six hundred and seventy and five: of the beeves, seventy and two: of the asses, sixty and one: and of the virgins, thirty and two.

33 And Moses delivered the tribute unto Eleazar, the priest, as an offering unto the Lord.

34 And Moses gave unto the congregation their portion: of the sheep, three hundred and seven and thirty thousand: of beeves, thirty and six thousand: of asses, thirty thousand and five hundred: and of virgins, sixteen thousand.

35 But of these the tribute unto the Lord, were of the sheep, six hundred and seventy and five: of the beeves, seventy

A. M. 2552.

and two: of the asses, sixty and one: and of the virgins, thirty and two.

36 And Moses delivered the tribute unto Eleazar, the priest, as an offering unto the Lord.

37 So the Lord's portion of the spoil delivered unto the Levites, were of the sheep, one thousand three hundred and fifty: of the beeves, one hundred and forty and two: of the asses, one hundred twenty and two: and of virgins, sixty and four: besides their part as one of the tribes of Israel.

38 But of the gold, and of the silver, and of the jewels, and of the chains, and of the bracelets, and of the ear-rings, which the men of war had taken, brought they unto Moses, and unto Eleazar: and Eleazar offered them up as an oblation unto the Lord.

39 And the sum thereof, was sixteen thousand and seven hundred and fifty shekels.

40 ¶ And it came to pass on the morrow, that the children of the tribe of Gad, and of the tribe of Reuben, drew near unto Moses, and unto Eleazar, the priest, and unto the elders of Israel, and said:

41 Behold our inheritance is fallen unto us on this side [f]Jordan.

42 And we, our wives, our children, and the virgins, the Lord hath given us, are many in number, and our cattle are a great multitude.

43 [g]Ataroth, [h]Dibon, [i]Jazer, with all the cites and villages on this side Jordan, in the land of Gilead, permit us to possess, that we may build sheep-folds for our cattle, and dwellings for our wives, and for our children.

44 And Moses said unto the rulers of the tribes of Reuben, and of Gad, Surely, to excuse yourselves from the war, from driving out the Canaanites, do ye ask of me this thing!

45 And they answered Moses and said, We, ourselves, will go armed unto the war, and we will pass over Jordan: neither will we return again unto our wives, and our children, until Israel hath possessed the land of Canaan.

46 And Moses said, Be it unto you even as you have said:

47 Only observe you this thing, that ye be ready to pass over Jordan armed before the Lord, and before Joshua, his servant, until he hath driven out your enemies: then shall ye return, and ye shall be guiltless before the Lord.

48 But if ye turn your backs on the covenant ye have this day made, behold the sin, which ye shall sin before the Lord, will avenge you.

49 And they said unto Moses: We, thy servants, will do as thou, our lord, hast commanded.

50 And they departed.

A. M. 2552.

[f] *Heb.* water of judgment.

[g] *Heb.* the horn of plenty.

[h] *Heb.* intelligent.

[i] *Heb.* helping.

A. M. 2553.

CHAP. XXVI.

1 *Joshua is appointed to succeed Moses.* 2 *Moses' charge to Joshua.* 15 *Moses blesses the tribes of Israel.* 27 *Takes the rod from Jasher.* 29 *He goes up Pisgah.* 30 *Views the promised land.* 32 *Moses dies.*

1 AND the Lord said unto Moses, Call Joshua, the son of Nun, unto you, before the door of the tabernacle of the congregation, and give unto him a charge; for behold the days draw nigh wherein thou shalt die.

2 And Moses did as the Lord commanded, and Moses said unto Joshua in the sight of all Israel, Thus saith the Lord, Be strong, and of great courage, for thee have I chosen to lead my people into the land of which I sware unto them, that they should possess it; and I will be with thee.

3 ¶ And the Lord spake unto Moses, and said, Write now a song, even the song I shall teach thee, that the children of Israel may learn the words thereof; that they may not hereafter forsake my laws, nor disregard the statutes which they have received.

4 And Moses spake before the congregation all the words of the song, until they were ended.

5 And Moses spake unto Joshua, and unto Eleazar, the priest, saying, Lay up before the Lord, in the ark of the covenant, the words which this day I have taught the children of Israel, that your sons, and your sons' sons, and your daughters, may learn them.

A. M. 2553.

6 And Moses, and the children of Israel, sojourned in the plains of Moab, by Jordan, over against Jericho.

7 ¶ And Moses assembled together Joshua, and all the children of Israel, and he said unto them:

8 Behold the days draw nigh wherein I shall be gathered unto my fathers.

9 And thus saith the Lord, When ye shall pass over Jordan into the land of Canaan, that ye shall drive out the inhabitants: and ye shall divide by lot, their land among your families: according to the number of each tribe, shall ye divide it.

10 Ye shall surely drive out the inhabitants, none shall remain, lest Israel be corrupted through their abominations, and they be as thorns in your sides.

11 And these are the men who shall divide the land: even Eleazar, the priest, and Joshua, the son of Nun.

12 And of the princes of the people, Caleb, [a]Shemuel, [b]Elidad, [c]Bukki, [d]Hanniel, [e]Kemuel, [f]Elizaphan, [g]Paltiel, [h]Ahihud, and [i]Pedahel.

13 And thus saith the Lord, Command the children of Is-

[a] *Heb.* established.
[b] *Heb.* beloved of the Lord.
[c] *Heb.* dispersed.
[d] *Heb.* grace of God.
[e] *Heb.* the raised of God.
[f] *Heb.* the inspector.
[g] *Heb.* liberty.
[h] *Heb.* brother of praise.
[i] *Heb.* popular.

A. M. 2553.

rael, that they give unto the Levites, forty and eight cities, for them to dwell therein.

14 And the suburbs thereof shall measure two thousand cubits on the north, on the south, on the east, and on the west, of every city: and every city shall be in the midst thereof.

15 ¶ Then Moses blessed the tribes of Israel, and he said:

16 O that Reuben may live, and become a great people!

[k] *Heb.* thanksgiving.

17 That [k] Judah may be sufficient, that his enemies do not spoil him.

18 Of Levi, he shall possess Urim and Thummim; the Lord shall smite through the loins of them that rise up against him: for they shall teach Jacob the statutes of the Lord, and they shall offer burnt-offerings and incense before the Lord, for ever.

[l] *Heb.* dexterous

19 [l] Benjamin shall be the beloved of the Lord: under the shadow of the Almighty shall be his safety.

20 Joseph shall receive of the precious things of the firmament, he shall eat of the fat of the land, and shall be satisfied: his glory shall be the strength as of a unicorn; he shall push the people together unto the ends of the earth.

[m] *Heb.* inhabiting.
[n] *Heb.* commerce

21 [m] Zebulun and [n] Issachar shall rejoice: they shall suck of the plenty of the seas, and of the hidden things of the sand.

A. M. 2553.

[o] *Heb.* a host.

22 [o] Gad shall dwell as a lion: he shall judge among the people, and the people shall bless him.

23 Dan shall thrive as a lion's whelp: his habitation shall be from Bashan.

[p] *Heb.* wrestled.

24 [p] Naphtali shall be highly favoured; and shall be filled with the blessings of the Lord.

[q] *Heb.* subtle.

25 [q] Ashur shall be blessed with his children: his foot shall he dip in oil, his shoes shall be iron and brass, and as his days, so shall his strength be.

[r] *Heb.* hearing.

26 [r] Simeon shall be many for number: and his bread shall be fatness.

27 ¶ And Moses called for Eleazar, the priest, and he said unto him: Take now from Jasher, the rod, and do thou lay it up before the Lord in the tabernacle of the congregation, on the side of the mercy-seat shall it be laid up.

28 And I, Jasher, the son of Caleb, delivered unto Eleazar, the priest, the rod: and Eleazar put it up in the tabernacle, on the side of the mercy-seat before the ark: and it remaineth there even unto this day.

29 ¶ And when Moses had made an end of blessing the children of Israel, he went up out of the plains of Moab, unto mount [s] Nebo, even unto the top of [t] Pisgah.

[s] *Heb.* fruitful.
[t] *Heb.* lofty.

A. M. 2553.

[u] *Heb.* testifying.
[x] *Heb.* forgetting
[y] *Heb.* moonshine.

30 And from thence he saw all the land of [u] Gilead, even unto Dan and [x] Manasseh, and the land of Judah, even unto the sea, the plain of the valley of [y] Jericho, and the city of the palm-trees, even unto Zoar.

31 And he said, Now behold I with my eyes the land, concerning which the Lord sware unto Abraham, Isaac, and Jacob, saying, I will give it unto thy seed.

32 And Moses died in the land of Moab.

33 And Moses was an hundred and twenty years old when he died.

34 And the children of Israel wept for Moses thirty days.

CHAP. XXVII.

1 *Joshua exhorts the people to pass over Jordan.* 8 *He sends messengers to Rahab, a princess of Jericho.* 14 *Rahab, her advice to the king of Jericho.* 19 *It is rejected.*

2554. 1 NOW it came to pass, after the days of weeping for Moses were ended, on the morrow thereof, that Joshua assembled Eleazar, the priest, and all the elders of the people, with the captains over thousands, over hundreds, over fifties, and over twenties, before the door of the tabernacle of the congregation.

2 And Joshua said, Moses, the servant of the Lord, said unto me: When I am gathered unto my fathers, then shalt thou lead the people over Jordan into the land of Canaan: and the Lord will be with thee, and will fight for thee. A. M. 2554.

3 Prepare therefore for your journey; arm yourselves for the battle: for lo! the trumpet shall sound on the third day, and the ark of the Lord shall go over Jordan before the people.

4 ¶ Then spake unto Joshua the chief of the tribes of Reuben, Gad, and Manasseh, We remember the covenant we made with Moses, the servant of the Lord; we will go over Jordan armed, and we will not return until our brethren have found rest.

5 And all the elders with one voice cried out and said, All things wherein we obeyed Moses, the servant of the Lord, and listened unto his voice, will we now do.

6 And whosoever shall turn his back on whatsoever thou commandest, he shall surely die.

7 ¶ And it came to pass on the third day, on the morning thereof, that Joshua rose up early, and the trumpet sounded, and the people gathered themselves together, and they removed from [a] Shittim, and they came unto Jordan, and they pitched there. [a] *Heb.* lodged

8 And Joshua sent messengers unto [b] Rahab, one of [b] *Heb.* generous.

A. M. 2554.

the princesses of Jericho, saying:

9 Behold, on the morrow we shall pass over Jordan, and the Lord will deliver Jericho into our hands.

10 And Rahab said unto those who were sent, Speak unto Joshua and say: The Lord, the God of Jacob, prosper you, inasmuch as I also am the daughter of an Israelite, by a woman of Midian.

11 And it was told unto the king of Jericho all the words which Rahab had spoken.

12 Then the king of Jericho assembled together all his princes and his nobles, and Rahab was there also, for she was a woman renowned for wisdom.

13 And the king said unto Rahab, How is this that you confederate with the avowed enemy of the nations?

14 And Rahab answered, and said, Let not the king be angry, and thy servant will speak:

15 Behold thus saith Rahab, I was born among the Israelites, and they are as the locusts for number, and the Lord, the maker of heaven and earth, [r]whom thou knowest not, he fighteth for them, even for Joshua, for Caleb, and for all Israel.

[r] *Or,* whom thou dost not worship.

16 And this, O king, thou knowest, that Moses, with a few chosen men, smote all the people of Midian, all the people of Moab, all the Jebusites, all the Hittites, all the Hivites, and all the Amorites on the other side Jordan, with the edge of the sword, save only the females, from whom Israel do and will hereafter multiply exceedingly;

17 And hath given their land unto the tribe of Reuben, unto the tribe of Gad, and unto the half-tribe of Manasseh.

18 Send messengers therefore unto Joshua, and say, Thus saith Jericho, Spare us, we beseech thee, you shall go quietly through our lands, you, your wives, your children, your flocks, and your herds, and ye shall eat of our bread, and drink of our vintage.

19 Peradventure the wrath of Joshua will be turned away from destroying thee, and thy people.

20 And the king of Jericho said, It is the counsel of an harlot; and Rahab was shut up in her own house, and spies were set, that they might watch her.

A. M. 2554.

CHAP. XXVIII.

1 *The ark passeth over Jordan.* 8 *All Israel pass over Jordan in six days.* 15 *Rahab sends messengers to Joshua.* 17 *She dwells in Israel.* 18 *Jericho is taken.* 20 *Achan, his rebellion.*

1 AND it came to pass on the morrow, that Joshua spake unto Eleazar, the priest,

A. M. 2554.

and unto the Levites, saying,

2 Let the ark of the covenant of the Lord be borne before the people by the priests, as they pass over Jordan.

3 Only this I command, that the tribe of Reuben, the tribe of Gad, and the half-tribe of Manasseh, shall pass over armed first; even as Moses hath commanded.

4 Moreover, no one shall come nigh unto the ark: fifty cubits shall the children of Israel, except the priests, leave between them and the ark.

5 And the trumpet sounded, and the tribe of Reuben, the tribe of Gad, and the half-tribe of Manasseh, even all the males thereof, from sixteen years of age, and upwards, passed over Jordan, armed.

6 Then followed the ark of the covenant of the Lord, borne by the priests, and they passed over in the midst thereof.

7 And there followed the tribe of Benjamin, even all the armed men thereof, their wives, their children, their flocks, and their herds.

8 And in six days the whole congregation of the children of Israel passed over Jordan, they, their wives, their children, their cattle, even all their possessions.

9 And they encamped on the west of Jordan, in the plains of Jericho.

A. M. 2554.

10 And the wood whereon the children of Israel passed over Jordan, stayed upon the face of the waters six days and six nights.

11 And when the people of Jericho, and the kings of the land of Canaan, had heard that Joshua, and all the children of Israel, had passed over Jordan, and were encamped in the plains of Jericho, great fear fell upon them.

12 ¶ Now after the people had rested seven days, Joshua commanded the captains of thousands, the captains of hundreds, and the captains of fifties, saying:

13 Prepare ye for the war, that we go up and smite Jericho, and the king thereof, and all the inhabitants, with the edge of the sword.

14 And there came forth of all Israel, forty thousand men armed for the battle: and Joshua was magnified in the sight of the Amorites, in the sight of the Canaanites, and in the sight of all the nations.

15 Then Rahab sent unto Joshua, saying: Let me intreat with thee for my nation, that they may live.

16 And Joshua answered, and said, As many as save themselves by flight, may live: but whosoever shall be found in Jericho, shall surely die the death.

17 Then came Rahab, with her kindred, and with all her

A. M. 2554.

household, unto Joshua; and she dwelleth with the children of Israel unto this day.

18 And the people of Jericho fled from the city, every one to the mountains.

19 And Joshua took the gold and the silver, even all the spoil of Jericho; and he brought it into the treasury of the Lord, and it was holy.

20 ¶ And [a]Achan spake aloud, and said, Wherefore hath Joshua taken from the congregation, all the gold, all the silver, and all the brass; even all the spoil of the city of Jericho, and given it to the tribe of Levi.

[a] *Heb.* winebibber.

21 Moses, the servant of the Lord, when we slew the Midianites, the Moabites, and the people of the nations, on the other side Jordan, gave the half of the spoil unto the armed men, who went forth to the battle, and the other half he gave unto the congregation, according to their tribes.

22 And the sayings of Achan were told unto Joshua, and Joshua said to the Levites:

23 Bring forth Achan, and let him be stoned, for he hath blasphemed.

24 And they stoned Achan in the valley of [b]Achor, in the presence of Joshua, and of the elders, until he was dead.

[b] *Heb.* tumult.

25 And thus did Joshua punish the rebellion of Achan, even as the Lord had commanded.

A. M. 2555.

CHAP. XXIX.

1 Joshua goeth up to Ai. 5 Five thousand Israelites lie in ambush. 11 Ai is taken. 13 The king of Ai hanged. 17 The Gibeonites become the servants of Joshua.

1 AND it came to pass on the morrow, that Joshua arose, with the men of war, even thirty thousand men of valour.

2 And Joshua said, Go up against [a]Ai, and smite the inhabitants thereof with the edge of the sword: let none escape alive.

[a] *Heb.* woe.

3 And they went forth, and they abode between [b]Bethel and Ai: and Joshua lodged among the people that night.

[b] *Heb.* the house of God.

4 And Joshua arose up early, he, and the elders, and they went up to Ai.

5 And Joshua took about five thousand men, and he commanded them to lie in ambush on the west side of Ai.

6 And when the captains had set the people, even all the host of Israel, Joshua went that night into the midst of the valley.

7 And when the king of Ai saw all that was done, but he knew not of the men who lay in ambush, he sent messengers unto Joshua, saying:

8 On the morrow, about noon, I, and the men that are with me, will give you, and thy people, battle in the plain.

A. M. 2555.

9 Then said Joshua unto the captains, and unto the people: Behold, when the king of Ai, and his people, come forth to the battle, seem ye as if ye fled before them for fear: and flee ye by the way of the wilderness.

10 So shall it come to pass, that the men of Ai shall come forth of their city, and when the trumpet shall sound, then shall ye turn upon the men of Ai, and destroy them. And they did so.

11 And those five thousand men who lay in ambush, arose and entered Ai, and took it, and all the spoil thereof.

12 And when the men of Ai saw all that was done, and that they had no power to flee this way or that way, they were sore troubled.

13 And Joshua, and the people, smote the men of Ai, and chased them in the field, and pursued them into the wilderness, until there remained none of them, save the king of Ai, whom Joshua hanged on a tree.

14 And Joshua went up to Ai, and smote it with the edge of the sword, all the men, the women, and all the children thereof, save the virgin who knew not man.

15 Then Joshua took all their cattle, and the spoil of their city, as a prey for Israel, as the Lord had commanded Moses.

16 ¶ Now it came to pass, after Joshua had smote Jericho and Ai, two great cities of Canaan, that great fear fell upon the Gibeonites. A. M. 2556.

17 And they sent messengers unto Joshua to [c]Gilgal, saying: We are thy servants; whatsoever thou shalt command us, that will we do.

18 Only this we pray thee, do not unto us as thou hast done unto the men of Jericho, and unto the men of Ai.

19 Then said Joshua unto the messengers, This shall ye do, ye shall live, and ye shall fight for us, and we will fight for you: so shall it come to pass, that ye shall live quietly in the land.

20 ¶ And the Gibeonites dwelt in [d]Gibeon, which is a great city, and a royal city, and much greater than Ai: and the men thereof, were more mighty.

[c] *Heb.* round.

[d] *Heb.* my town.

CHAP. XXX.

1 *Five kings war against Gibeon.* 5 *Joshua fighteth for Gibeon;* 9 *and overcometh the five kings;* 14 *and afterwards destroyeth their cities.* 18 *Other kings war against Joshua.* 25 *Joshua putteth them to flight.*

1 NOW when all the kings which dwell on this side 2557.
Jordan, and on the coasts of the great sea, with [a]Adonizedek, king of Jerusalem, had heard all the mighty works which Joshua had done, and

[a] *Heb.* the just lord.

A. M. 2557.

that the men of Gibeon had made a league with him, that they were moved.

2 Wherefore Adonizedek sent unto [b]Hoham, king of Hebron, and unto [c]Piram, king of [d]Jarmuth, and unto [e]Japhia, king of [f]Lachish, and unto [g]Debir, king of [h]Eglon, saying,

3 Come up unto me, that we, and the kings which dwell on this side Jordan, and the kings of the sea-coast, may fight against Gibeon, and destroy it, because the men thereof have made peace with Joshua, and with all Israel.

4 Therefore the five kings of the Amorites, the king of Jerusalem, the king of Hebron, the king of Jarmuth, the king of Lachish, and the king of Eglon, gathered themselves together, and went up, they, and all their hosts: and they encamped before Gibeon, and they made war against it.

5 ¶ Now Joshua was at this time at Gilgal, with all the armed men of Israel.

6 And the men of Gibeon sent unto Joshua, saying, Because we are thy servants, behold all the nations on this side Jordan have waged war against us.

7 Come up therefore quickly unto us, and help us, and save us, thy servants, that we perish not.

8 And Joshua hasted from Gilgal, with all the men of war, and the mighty men of valour.

9 And he came suddenly upon them before the break of day, and he discomfited them, and they fled: and he slew them with a great slaughter before Gibeon, and he chased them along the way that goeth up to [i]Beth-horon, and he smote them even unto [k]Azekah, and unto [l]Makkedah.

10 And Joshua pursued them with great slaughter until the evening.

11 And Joshua said, Sun, be thou silent upon Gibeon: and thou, moon, shine thou on the valley of [m]Ajalon.

12 And Joshua returned; and all the men of war with him, to Gilgal.

13 And the Gibeonites returned to their city: and they rejoiced greatly.

14 ¶ And it came to pass, after Joshua, and the men of Israel, had rested themselves at Gilgal, that he sent chosen men up against Makkedah, against Lachish, against Debir, against Jarmuth, against [n]Libnah, and against [o]Gezer.

15 And they fought against them, and they took them, even all the cities; and he did unto them, even as he had done unto Jericho, and unto Ai: and he slew the kings thereof, and all the inhabitants thereof, with the edge of the sword: even all the men, the women, and the children, save the virgin

A. M. 2557.

[b] *Heb.* woe to them.
[c] *Heb.* fierce.
[d] *Heb.* haughtiness.
[e] *Heb.* resplendent.
[f] *Heb.* walking place.
[g] *Heb.* oracle.
[h] *Heb.* rotund.
[i] *Heb.* house of the sun.
[k] *Heb.* walled.
[l] *Heb.* burnt.
[m] *Heb.* strong as an oak.
[n] *Heb.* bright as the moon.
[o] *Heb.* cut off.

A. M. 2557.

who knew not man, by lying with him.

16 And the fame thereof went out throughout all the land of Canaan, and the kings of the mountains, and the kings of the valleys, and the kings of the sea-shore, assembled themselves together, and said,

17 Surely as dead men are we before Joshua, and before the men of Israel.

18 And [p]Jabin, king of [q]Hazor, said unto [r]Jobab, king of [s]Madon, and unto the kings of the sea-shore: Up, let us gather together our hosts, our armies, and our chariots, and let us assemble together at the waters of [t]Merom, and fight against Israel, and destroy them, lest they slay us, our wives, and our sons, and take from us our daughters, and our heritages.

19 And the words of Jabin were acceptable unto all who heard them.

20 And they gathered themselves together at the waters of Merom, and they were much people; even as the sand upon the sea-shore for multitude: and they defied the armies of Israel.

21 And Jabin stood forth and said, Know ye this, if it should come to pass, that the Israelites prevail this day, then shall all the nations be slain: or we; and our sons, shall become the vassals and slaves of the Hebrews.

22 For this cause came they out of Egypt, to slay, and dispossess, according to all that the lawgiver, even Moses, hath commanded them.

23 To take from us our cities, our lands, our vineyards, our cattle, our gold, our silver, our brass, and also our pure virgins.

24 And lo! now Joshua, and the people of war that are with him, come forth to the battle.

25 And Joshua, with forty and two thousand men, with the men of Gibeon, came suddenly upon them, and slew them, and chased them to Zidon, and he smote them until there were none remaining.

26 And Joshua burnt Hazor, because of Jabin, the king thereof; for he it was who led the nations to battle.

27 And all the rest of the cities saved Joshua, but the spoil thereof reserved he as a prey for the children of Israel.

28 Then Joshua wared against the Anakims; and he left none of them, save in [u]Gaza, in [x]Gath, and [y]Ashdod.

29 And the land rested from war.

[p] *Heb.* knowing
[q] *Heb.* the granary.
[r] *Heb.* howling.
[s] *Heb.* reproof.
[t] *Heb.* high-minded.
[u] *Heb.* strong as a goat.
[x] *Heb.* rest.
[y] *Heb.* fire of the beloved.

CHAP. XXXI.

1 *Joshua is stricken in years.* 4 *He divides Canaan.* 12 *The borders of the several tribes* 24 *Israel enjoys peace and plenty.*

1 AND it came to pass after many days, that Joshua spake unto Eleazar, the 2559.

A. M. 2559. priest, unto Caleb, and unto all the elders, and unto the congregation of the children of Israel, saying:

2 Behold I am grown old, and am stricken in years: and peradventure the days draw nigh wherein I shall be gathered unto my fathers.

3 And all that Moses, the servant of the Lord, hath said unto me, that hath the Lord done by me.

4 Unto the tribe of Reuben, the tribe of Gad, and the half-tribe of Manasseh, did Moses, whilst he was yet with us, give all the land on the west of Jordan, the land of the Amorites, the land of Moab, the land of Midian, all Bashan, and half of Gilead; even all the nations which the Lord delivered into his hands.

5 And at that time, Moses spake unto me and said, When ye shall pass over Jordan, and the Lord shall deliver into your hands all the land of Canaan, to possess it, that ye shall divide the land by lot unto the nine tribes, and unto the half-tribe of Manasseh.

6 And Caleb stood forth, and said unto Joshua: Lo! Caleb, thy servant, is now fourscore and nine years old.

7 And these fifty and eight years have I gone forth to the battle, with the bow, with the spear, and with the javelin.

8 The tribe of Judah is a great tribe, and Moses, the servant of the Lord, hath said, A. M. 2559.
when he sent me to spy out the land, Surely the land on which thy feet have trodden, shall be thine inheritance, and thy children's, for ever.

9 And behold I am as strong this day as I was on that day in which Moses sent me: as was my strength then, so is it now for war, both to go out, and to come in.

10 And behold, though the Anakims dwell in the land, give it unto me, that I may possess it: then shall I be able to drive them out.

11 And Joshua said, Be it unto you, even as thou hast said: and he blessed him.

12 ¶ So the border of the lot of Judah encompassed the salt sea at the end of Jordan, and fetched a compass by Kadesh Barnea: even by Karkaa, unto Hazor, even unto the river of Egypt.

13 And from Gaza, even to Ashdod, were its borders on the great sea.

14 And from Ashdod it fetched a compass: and its borders went out by Gath, even unto Makkedah.

15 And from thence the border went out by Bethshemosh, unto the south side of the Jebusite, even unto Debir, did it go.

16 This is the coast of the children of the tribe of Judah round about, according to their lot.

A. M. 2559.

17 ¶ Then spake Joshua and said, The lot of the children of Joseph shall be from Jordan by Jericho, to Bethel, and Luz, and Ataroth, and Gezer, and all the cities, and plains, and the lands thereof.

18 But the elders of the tribe of Joseph, said unto Joshua, Give, we pray thee, the land thou hast allotted for us unto [a] Ephraim: for we be many.

[a] *Heb.* fruitful.

19 Let us go up to the wood-country, and cut down the trees thereof, that we may drive out the Perizzites, that we may have cities and houses to dwell in, and lands whereon to feed our flocks and our herds.

20 And Joshua said, Go, and do as ye have spoken: and he blessed them.

21 ¶ And Joshua divided all the land of Canaan, to every tribe, according to its number, even as Moses had commanded him.

22 Only to the tribe of Levi did he give no inheritance: for the priesthood is their portion, save the forty and eight cities for them to dwell in.

23 Joshua appointed also cities of refuge for the slayer, throughout all the tribes of Israel.

24 And the children of Israel had peace: and they were filled with plenty, with riches, and with virgins.

CHAP. XXXII.

A. M. 2560.

1 *Circumcision renewed.* 13 *Joshua dismisses the tribes of Reuben, Gad, and Manasseh.* 18 *They return, and repass Jordan.*

1 NOW it came to pass in those days, that Joshua assembled together Eleazar, the priest, the Levites, and all the congregation at Shiloh, and he set up the tabernacle of the Lord there.

2 And Joshua stood before the door of the tabernacle of the congregation: and he spake in the presence of all Israel, and he said,

3 Now behold the Lord hath given you rest in the land concerning which he sware unto your fathers, saying, Thy seed shall inherit the land of Canaan.

4 Abraham, our father, heard a voice, when he dwelt in this land, which said unto him: Circumcise the flesh of thy foreskin, for therefore art thou barren.

5 When your fathers were in bondage in Egypt, because of the Egyptians from the time of the birth of Moses, they were uncircumcised.

6 But Moses, the servant of the Lord, commanded me, saying, When ye be come into the land of Canaan, to possess it, speak unto the Levites, and say:

7 Make unto yourselves razors, and let the priests circum-

A. M. 2560 cise one the other: and circumcise ye all the males of the children of Israel.

8 And the Levites did so: and all the people abode in their tents in the camp till they were whole.

9 And Joshua said, This shall be a law and an ordinance unto you, to be observed in all your tribes, and in all your families.

10 Ye shall bring every male on the eighth day after he openeth the womb, unto the priest, to be circumcised: ye shall do this, both ye, your sons, and your sons' sons, for ever.

11 And it came to pass after seven days, that the people were whole.

12 Then Joshua commanded Eleazar, the priest, and he read out of the book of the covenant, all the laws, and the ordinances which Moses commanded to be observed, concerning the servant, whether he be an Hebrew, or a stranger, and the statutes concerning the virgins of the nations, and the children born unto them.

13 And Joshua blessed the tribe of Reuben, the tribe of Gad, and the half-tribe of Manasseh, and he said unto them:

14 Return ye by the way ye came, and go over Jordan, unto you wives, unto your sons, unto your daughters, and unto your flocks, and unto your possessions.

15 For ye have done all that Moses hath commanded you: ye have obeyed me also. A. M. 2560.

16 But take ye diligent heed to do the commandments and the laws of the Lord; to cleave unto him; and to serve him with all your heart; and with all your soul.

17 Then the tribe of Reuben, the tribe of Gad, and the half-tribe of Manasseh, even all the armed men thereof, departed from Joshua, at [a]Shiloh. [a] *Heb.* disbanding.

18 And they passed over Jordan, to the land of Gilead, whereof they were possessed, as Moses had spoken.

19 And the tribe of Reuben, the tribe of Gad, and the half-tribe of Manasseh, returned into the land of Gilead, with their shares of the spoil they had taken from the Canaanites, with much cattle, with gold, with silver, with iron, and with brass, and with very much raiment: and with their portion of pure virgins; as the Lord had commanded Moses.

CHAP. XXXIII.

1 *The Reubenites, the Gadites, and the Manassites build a tabernacle and an altar.* 5 *Joshua is angry with them.* 8 *Joshua sends Phinehas to them.* 15 *Their reasons.* 22 *Joshua is pacified.* 29 *Joshua and Eleazar die.*

1 NOW it came to pass 2561.
that the elders of the

A. M. 2561. Reubenites, the elders of the Gadites, and the elders of the half-tribe of Manasseh, said one among another.

2 Behold Joshua, and our brethren, have set up the tabernacle in Shiloh; let us likewise build a tabernacle and an altar, as testimonies unto the Lord; for Jordan is a border between them and us.

3 That the Levites, who dwell among us, may offer up our burnt-offerings, our sacrifices, and our peace-offerings, unto the Lord.

4 And they built a tabernacle, and they sat up an altar on this side Jordan, in the land of their possession, even in Gilead.

5 ¶ And it came to pass, when Joshua and the children of Israel heard thereof, that they assembled themselves together at Shiloh.

6 And Phinehas said, Lo! the people of Reuben, the people of Gad, with the Manassites, seek to make themselves a separate people; even as Korah, have they sinned.

7 For they have built a tabernacle, and they have set up an altar, on the other side Jordan; unto Shiloh will they not come, at the place which the Lord hath appointed will they not appear, to offer sacrifices and burnt-offerings.

8 And Joshua said, Send Phinehas, Caleb, and Jasher, with the princes of Israel; and let them pass over Jordan, and enquire at their hands the cause thereof. A. M. 2561.

9 And they went, and they passed over Jordan: and they saw the tabernacle and the altar which the children of Reuben, the children of Gad, and the children of Manasseh, had built, and behold they were well to look unto.

10 And they said unto the Reubenites, the Gadites, and the Manassites, Wherefore have ye thus trespassed in making yourselves a people to rebel against the Lord?

11 Tell us, we pray ye, Wherefore have ye built a tabernacle and an altar, besides the tabernacle and the altar which are in Shiloh?

12 And the men of Reuben, the men of Gad, and the men of Manasseh, answered, and said, The Lord, the God of our fathers, knoweth, that as a testimony have we built the tabernacle and the altar.

13 For Jordan is between us and Shiloh; wherefore that we, our wives, our sons, and our daughters, might worship the Lord, surely have we done this thing.

14 And speak unto Joshua, and unto our brethren on the other side of the river of Jordan, and say,

15 Thus say the men of Reuben, the men of Gad, and the men of Manasseh, As the Lord liveth, we, and our sons,

A. M. 2561. from sixteen years of age, shall appear once in every year before the Lord, in Shiloh.

16 Moreover, whatsoever ye shall command us, that will we do.

17 And the words of the Reubenites, of the Gadites, and of the Manassites, were pleasing unto Phinehas, and unto all those who were with him.

18 ¶ Then Caleb, Phinehas, Jasher, with the princes, returned unto Joshua, and unto the children of Israel, in Shiloh.

19 And they said, Thus say our brethren, the men of Reuben, the men of Gad, and the men of Manasseh, We are the people of the Lord: and as a testimony thereof have we built for us, our wives, our sons, and our daughters, a tabernacle, and have set up an altar.

20 And behold once in every year will we, and our sons, from sixteen years, and upwards, appear before the Lord, in Shiloh.

21 And whatsoever ye shall command us, that will we do.

22 And the thing pleased Joshua, and all Israel; and they said, We will not destroy the land wherein the children of Reuben, of Gad, and of Manasseh, dwell.

23 And they said, Their chosen men shall bear testimony also among the elders of Israel, at Shiloh.

24 Now had Israel rest from A. M.
all their enemies round about: 2561.
for the people of the nations feared greatly.

25 ¶ And Joshua waxed old, and he called for all Israel, and he said: Behold, I have divided unto you, by lot, all the land of Canaan, as an inheritance for your tribes, possess ye the land, as the Lord hath promised unto you.

26 Now, therefore, fear ye the Lord: and serve him in sincerity, and in truth.

27 And the people said unto Joshua, We will serve the Lord.

28 And when Joshua had made an end of speaking, the people departed, each man to his dwelling.

29 And Joshua died, being 2561.
one hundred and ten years of age.

30 And Eleazar, the son of Aaron, died.

CHAP. XXXIV.

1 *Judah and Simeon take possession of their lots.* 4 *Othniel smiteth Kirjaeth-sepher.* 7 *The Israelites suffer the Canaanites to dwell among them.* 15 *Phinehas reproves the Israelites for so doing.* 21 *The people weep.* 21 *Caleb dies.*

1 NOW after the death of 2565.
Joshua, Judah said to Simeon, Come thou, and let us drive out the Canaanite out of my lot: and I will go with thee up into thy lot.

A. M. 2565.

2 And they did so: and they slew of the Canaanites, ten thousand men.

3 ¶ And Caleb said, He that smiteth Kirjaeth-sepher: to him will I give [a] Achsah, my daughter, to wife.

4 And [b] Othniel, the younger brother of Caleb, took it: then gave he unto him Achsah, his daughter.

5 And the children of Judah said unto the Kenites, Ye are the children of Jethro, who was father-in-law to Moses, ye shall dwell in the land, and ye shall fight for us, and we will fight for you.

6 Then Judah went up with Simeon into his lot: and he took Gaza, [c] Askalon, [d] Ekron, and the mountains.

7 But the inhabitants of the valleys he could not drive out, nor the Jebusites that dwell in Jerusalem: wherefore they dwell among them even to this day.

8 Joseph also in his lot did not drive out the Canaanites: but the Canaanites still dwell among them.

9 Manasseh in his lot did not utterly drive them out: for the Canaanites would dwell in Megiddo, Dor, Taanach, and Bethshean.

10 Neither did Ephraim drive out the Canaanites: but they dwelt with them in Gezer.

11 The children of Zebulun made the inhabitants of Kitron and Nahaleel their tributaries.

A. M. 2565.

12 The children of Ashur also dwell among the Canaanites, the inhabitants of the land: in Accho, Zidon, Ahlab, Achzib, Helbah, Aphik, and Rehob.

13 Neither did Napthali drive out the Canaanites: nevertheless made they the inhabitants of Bethshemosh and of Beth-anath tributaries.

14 So also the tribe of Dan dwelt among the Canaanites.

2568.

15 ¶ And it came to pass, when the tribes of the children of Israel had gone up each unto his lot, that Phinehas, the priest, spake unto the elders of the people, and said:

16 What is this that you have done? Moses, the servant of the Lord, said unto you, Ye shall surely drive out all the inhabitants of the land.

17 And behold ye have made a league with the Canaanites, with the Jebusites, with the Perrizzites, and with the Amorites: and ye dwell among them.

18 And the elders of the people said, They were too strong for us: peradventure if we had not made a league with them, we had all perished, we, our wives, and our children, and all our flocks, and our herds, and our gold, and our silver, and our virgins; even all our possessions, had been a prey unto them.

[a] *Heb.* the enchanter.

[b] *Heb.* hour of the Lord.

[c] *Heb.* the balance.

[d] *Heb.* enervated.

A. M. 19 For who are they, now
2568. Moses and Joshua are dead,
who can lead forth all the
people to battle!
20 Then answered Phine-
has, and said, The Canaanites
will henceforth be as thorns
in your side, and their customs
will be as snares unto you: and
the Lord, the God of our fa-
thers, will not go forth with
our armies.
21 And the elders of the
people, lifted up their voice,
and wept: because of those
things, which should befall all
Israel.
22 ¶ Now Caleb ruled in
Israel after Joshua was dead,
twelve years.
23 And the people dwelt in
peace, all his days.
2575. 24 And Caleb died, and
was buried: and the children
of Israel mourned until the
thirtieth day.

CHAP. XXXV.

1 *Jasher succeeds Caleb, his father.* 7 *Jezer obtains leave to build a city.* 11 *Azuba, her complaint.* 14 *Ehud advises to slay the Canaanites.* 16 *The Israelites separate themselves from them.* 28 *Deborah, her request is granted.*

2576. 1 AND it came to pass af-
ter these things were
fulfilled, that Phinehas, and
the elders of the tribes of Is-
rael, assembled themselves to-
gether at Shiloh.
2 And they said, Who shall
judge Israel? for behold, now
Moses, Joshua, and Caleb, are A. M.
dead, the people of the Lord 2576.
are without a leader.
3 And they named Jasher,
the son of Caleb, by Azuba:
seeing he is an upright man.
4 And, moreover, this we
know, that he hath seen all the
wonders, wrought in Egypt,
in the wilderness: even all the
mighty works, that have been
done.
5 And the people shouted
for joy.
6 And Jasher judged Israel,
in Shiloh.
7 ¶ And it came to pass, 2577.
that [a]Jezer, his younger son, [a] *Heb.* dutiful.
said unto Jasher: Behold, I
pray thee, the land of Canaan,
how the people of the nations
mix with thy people.
8 Wherefore let thy son,
even thy son Jezer, build him
a city, after his name: that the
people of the land may be shut
out from among us.
9 And Jasher said: Be it
even as thou hast spoken.
10 And Jezer builded him
a city, in the tribe of Judah:
the same is the habitation of
the Jasherites, unto this day.
11 ¶ Now it came to pass, 2579.
when the elders of the chil-
dren of Israel were assembled
together at Shiloh, that Azuba,
the mother of Jasher, spake,
and said,
12 Lo! the nations will
swallow us up: the name of
our fathers will surely be for-
gotten.

A. M. 2579. 13 For the sons of Israel
defile themselves with the wo-
men of the nations: they have
forsaken the daughters of Ja-
cob.

[b] *Heb.* unity. 14 And [b]Ehud said, Up, let
us slay the people of the na-
tions: let us utterly drive them
out of the land of Canaan.

15 For so long as they be
among us, they will be a snare
unto us: and Israel shall be de-
filed.

16 Then spake Jezer, and
said, Separate yourselves from
among them: let the Canaan-
ites inhabit their cities, and
let us possess our cities.

17 So that they may not
come nigh unto us: nor that
we, nor our sons, draw nigh to
the people of the nations.

18 And Othniel stood forth,
and said, Would to God, it was
now with us, as it was in the
days of Moses, and Joshua,
when all Israel went forth to
the war: then might we drive
out the nations!

19 For behold! now the
armed men of each tribe are
for themselves, and for the lot
of their inheritance.

20 Moreover, it will hence-
forth behove us, that we per-
mit not all the males of Israel
at one time to appear before
the Lord in Shiloh, lest the
enemy noteth it.

21 Who shall lead Reuben
over Jordan: will Gad with
Manasseh now fight for us?

22 Then spake Jasher and
said: Hear, O my people, A. M. 2580.
hearken unto the words, of the
son of Caleb, by Azuba.

23 Peradventure, the people
of the nations, are too strong
for us: and who is there now,
of the sons of Jacob, that shall
conquer.

24 Reject not, therefore the
counsels of Othniel, and of Je-
zer. Suffer ye the Canaanites,
the Perrizzites, the Hittites, the
Hivites, and the Amorites, to
dwell in their cities: and be-
sides the cities we possess of the
nations taken in the war, let us
build cities for our increase;
for our sons, and our daugh-
ters, and their children, that
they dwell therein, and serve
the Lord, the God of Abra-
ham, the God of Isaac, and
the God of Jacob, who hath
brought us out, from under the
bondage of Egypt, unto the
promised land: a land flowing
with milk, and with honey.

25 So shall we, and those
who come after us, be a sepa-
rate people: sanctified unto the
Lord.

26 Moreover, thus hath said
the Lord, by the mouth of his
servant Moses, Your sons shall
not take to wife the daughters
of the children of Canaan; lest
they be cut off from the con-
gregation.

27 And all the elders of Is-
rael cried out, and said, As
Jasher, our judge, hath spoken,
so shall it be.

28 ¶ Then came [a]Deborah, 2581.

[a] *Heb.* the word; truth.

A. M. the daughter of Jasher, and
2581. said unto her father: Behold
my husband was slain before
Makkedah, when Israel went
out to fight for the people of
Gibeon.

28 Wherefore that I, and my sons, and my daughters, may serve the Lord, let us build us a city, that we may dwell therein.

30 And Jasher said, Thou hast said it: and call thou its name Debir.

CHAP. XXXVI.

1 Jasher sends messengers unto the kings of Canaan. 6 He assembles them nigh Bethel. 8 Jasher and the kings make a league. 15 The Israelites serve the Lord, all the days of Jasher.

2582. 1 AND it came to pass in
those days, that Jasher
sent messengers unto all the
kings, and unto all the nations
of Canaan: and he wrote unto them, saying:

2 Jasher, the judge of all Israel, unto the kings of the sea-coasts, the kings of the mountains, and the kings of the valleys, greeting: Know ye, that Moses, the servant of the Lord, hath commanded us, that we should not dwell with you in your cities, nor follow after your customs: and that we should not suffer you to dwell with us in our cities.

3 Seeing we worship the Lord, who made heaven, and
earth, and all things therein: A. M.
and ye fall down, and worship, 2582.
Baalim, and the gods of your
own imaginations.

4 That we shall not give our daughters unto your sons, nor take your daughters for our sons.

5 Wherefore thus saith Jasher, It behoveth, that ye assemble yourselves together, at Bethel: that I, and all the elders of Israel, may covenant with you.

6 ¶ And in those days, the 2583.
kings and princes of the sea-
coasts, the kings of the mountains, and the kings of the valleys, assembled themselves together, nigh unto Bethel, in the way as thou goest up to Beth-horon.

7 And Jasher, and all the elders of the tribes of Israel, came there also.

8 And Jasher stood forth, and he spake unto all the kings of the sea-coasts, the kings of the mountains, and the kings of the valleys, and said: To live in peace surely, that there be no more war between us, our sons, and our sons' sons, are we now come.

6 Behold, now, O, ye nations! chuse you out in every tribe, the cities ye are willing to dwell in, and all those lands, and possessions, which shall be yours: and be ye unto yourselves.

10 That your families remain inhabiters of the land,

A. M. 2583.

and that ye eat the fruit of
your increase.

11 Then answered all the
kings of the sea-coasts, the
kings of the mountains, and
the kings of the valleys, and
they said: What thou, O Ja-
sher, judge of all Israel, hath
spoken, seemeth unto us good:
and all that thou commandest,
that will we do.

12 And they bowed down
before Jasher; and before all
the elders of Israel.

13 And they did all that
Jasher had spoken, and they
took them cities, lands, and
possessions, in every tribe:
even such as Jasher, and the
elders of Israel, had appointed
for them.

14 And the people of Israel
dwelt in their cities, and had
their lands, and their posses-
sions; and the people of the
nations dwelt in their cities,
and had their lands, and pos-
sessions: and they are separa-
ted even unto this day.

15 ¶ And the children of
Israel served the Lord all the
days of Jasher, who had seen
all the great works done for
Israel, in Egypt, and in the
wilderness.

16 And Israel rested from
war, all the days of Jasher:
observing all things written in
the book of the covenant, and
Israel did not defile themselves
with the women of the na-
tions.

A. M 2594

CHAP. XXXVII.

1 The Israelites build them synagogues in every city. 3 The priests read the covenant therein. 3 They build no altar. 6 Jasher appoints rulers of cities. 8 Various habits to be worn. 10 Jasher assembles the elders. 13 He reminds them of former things. 21 His charge to the elders. 23 Othniel is to succeed Jasher. 24 Jasher blesses Israel. 26 Jazer builds an ark; 28 in which Jasher lays up the book which he had wrote.

1 NOW it came to pass in
process of time, when the
children of Israel had built
them cities, and had gotten
them possessions, in the land of
Canaan, that they grew migh-
ty; and for number, they were
as the sand on the sea-shore.

2 And they built little taber-
nacles in every city; and in
every town.

3 And the priests and Le-
vites, on every sabbath-day,
read before the people of every
city, and of every town, the
law, and the statutes: and they
rehearsed, in the ears of all the
people, the mighty works that
were done in Egypt, and in the
wilderness.

4 But they sat up no altar,
neither did they offer burnt-of-
ferings, or peace-offerings, save
only at Shiloh.

5 But the children of Israel,
throughout all their tribes, kept
the passover, and the feasts; as
Moses had appointed.

A. M. 2595. 6 ¶ And Jasher appointed rulers of cities; and rulers of towns.

7 And the people dwelt in peace; and they walked uprightly.

2597. 8 ¶ And it came to pass, that Jasher spake unto all the children of Israel, before the door of the tabernacle of the congregation, and he said, The garments of the virgin, of the virgin betrothed, of the married woman, and of the widow, shall from henceforth note them as such, that ye may be chaste before the Lord, your God.

9 Likewise the garments of the young man, of the married man, and of the widower, shall note them as such, that ye may be blameless.

10 And they said, All these things will we, our wives, our sons, and our daughters, observe to do.

11 ¶ Now it came to pass,
2599. that Jasher assembled together Phinehas, the priest, and Othniel, and all the elders of Israel:

12 And Jasher spake unto them, and he said: Lo! the days of my life are many, and the time is at hand that I shall return to the place of my fathers;

13 Hear therefore the words of Jasher:

14 Call to mind the days of old; remember the times that are past.

15 Our father Jacob dwelt in Hebron in this land. A. M. 2599.

16 And there was a sore famine in Canaan.

17 Now Pharaoh, king of Egypt, had advanced Joseph, one of the sons of Jacob.

18 Wherefore went he into Egypt, and he dwelt in the land of Goshen; and he died there.

19 After the death of Jacob, the Egyptians oppressed your brethren.

20 Then came Moses from Midian, and delivered us out of bondage; and led us through the Red Sea into the wilderness.

21 And now behold this day, is fulfilled the prophecy of Abraham: Unto thy seed will I give this land.

22 Ye are for multitude a great people: and it shall come to pass, that if you observe the statutes, and ordinances, of the Lord, and walk uprightly, ye shall drive out the remnant of the Gentiles.

23 Wherefore I charge ye this day, that ye command your sons, that they do not take them wives of the nations: it is an abomination, it bringeth destruction.

24 And lo, Othniel! peradventure he shall judge Israel after I am no more.

25 And Jasher blessed Israel, and he said, The Lord, the God of Abraham, the God of Isaac, and the God of Ja-

A. M. cob, prosper your going-out,
2600. and your coming-in.
26 ¶ And it came to pass
on the morrow, that Jasher
called unto him, his sons, and
his daughters; and he blessed
them, and he said,
27 The days of my life are
one hundred and twelve years:
these are the days of my pil-
grimage.
28 And Jasher said, This
book which I have written,
ye shall neither add to, nor di-
minish from: it is thine, and thy
sons, to possess for ever.
29 That the elders of Is-
rael, and the children not yet
born, may read and praise the A. M.
Lord. 2600
30 ¶ And when Jasher had
made an end of speaking, he
called unto him Jazer, his
eldest son, and he said unto
him, Build now an ark, that I
may put therein this testimony:
and do thou lay it up in the
city of Jezer.
31 And Jazer builded an
ark of Gopher-wood, and he
brought it unto his father, and
Jasher put therein the book,
which he had written.
32 And Jazer laid it up in
the city of Jezer.

THE END OF THE BOOK OF JASHER.

NOTES.

IT cannot be conceived that the author who so admirably describes the most High by his name JEHÓVAH, could intend to exclude his divine agency in the work of Creation; and therefore, when he says, The ether moved upon the surface of the chaos, we must understand the ether as a subordinate agent, under the direction and influence of the first great cause. The term Ruach, signifies spirit, breath, or wind, but when the Elohim is added, it signifies the energetic power and influence of JEHOVAH, and frequently the Holy Spirit. This all-pervading energy first gave motion to the ether, this communicated it to the dull insensible matter of the chaos, put life and motion into it, and produced the separation of the elements of air and fire, from earth and water, so that the abyss fled before the face of the light, and divided between the light, and the darkness. The ether, or firmament above, and the earth below, at first, only a mass of matter, but, by the agency of the Divine Being, using subordinate means, at length, subsided by its various stratas, so as to form the terraqueous globe, the waters subsiding to their proper channels.

The opinions of the numerous theorists, such as Burnet, Whiston, and others, widely differ on the nature of the abyss. The one insisting that there was no visible sea, but that the waters formed the abyss in the centre of the earth; the other, that the waters from the beginning, formed their own channels. The sacred historian, Moses, and the author of this Chronicle, leave these matters without explanation, only in general terms, declaring the separation of the grosser matter, the earth, from the finer matter of air and water.

It appears, both from Moses and Jasher, that the creation of the sun and moon is a glorious display of the divine power, and that their utility in the system is of the first importance, the one to rule the light, and the other to rule the darkness.

The formation of the earth was followed by the production of vegetable and animal substances; the latter not being created until a provision was made for their subsistence, the beast and every creeping thing from the earth, the fishes from the waters, and the fowl from the ether; each after their kind, with the power of propagating their species, so as to continue their various orders, in perpetual succession, without any new act of creation. Herein the divine power and energy are displayed in a most excellent manner, and may induce a due obedience to that command, Let every thing that hath breath, praise the Lord.

When all these things were finished, although the distinct work of each day is not mentioned, it is evident that Jasher attributes all things to God, as their author. Then having formed this noble theatre of nature, he beheld it with approbation, and having prepared it as the habitation of some superior being to what hitherto existed, he created man. This act, from the expression used, intimates design and counsel; and Moses beautifully expresses it by the important words, "Let us make man in our own image." And again, after his creation, "So God made man in his own image." Both in his spiritual and corporal state, he was made a resemblance of the moral and political image of God, as well as of his immortality and eternity.

It is evident that man knew his Creator, and was impressed with awe of his Majesty, and reverence of his power and glory; but especially of the highest admiration of his bounty and goodness, of his favour and love. The impressions of Deity upon his mind, were those which produced confidence, love, joy, and delight; and rendered obedience, not only rational, but grateful and pleasing; no reluctancy, no hesitation, no delay: all was harmony, peace, and love; creation smiled in all its richest productions, man enjoyed them with innocence, and returned his homage, devotion, and obedience. *Editor.*

Notes on Chap. I.

ADAM was perfect in his generation, complete in his stature; of the most extensive knowledge, walking uprightly, and eschewing evil. Eve was perfect in her generation, amiable, and lovely to look unto; of modest behaviour, of consummate chastity; beautiful, walking uprightly, and hating iniquity. Between these two, there was no superiority, they were both made at one time, and they both had the same powers of knowledge. *Hur, out of the book of Aaron.*

Notes on Chap. II.

NOAH was the first who builded up a ship, a floating house, an ark, to remain upon the surface of the waters. With this he visited the opposite land, and improved fishing; and his sons after him transplanted themselves to distant lands. *Hur.*

At this time all the people of the earth spake one language, and lived in common; were of one mode, of one form, and of one way of life. *Hur.*

And it came to pass when the sons of Japhet saw that the land was burthened with people, by reason of the longevity of men at this time, and the number of children born unto them, and having now built themselves floating habitations, and invented the sail, they sought distant lands. *Hur.*

The sons of Japhet settled in that part of Asia the less, which lieth upon the Mediterranean. *Ben Zaddi.*

In the days of Peleg it came to pass, that men first began to inclose lands. He enacted the laws of property. He settled the bounds of families; he first gave particular inheritances; he grew an arbitrator; lands were given by him for cultivation; infringers hence became culpable of his displeasure; punishments, riches, pride, government, poverty, idleness, and rebellion, ensued. Thus, at this time, people, friends, were dispersed; different interests destroyed union; avarice arose. One, from distance of place, became stranger and enemy to the other; contests and local vices sprung up. Leaders, rulers, teachers, arose; new words and ideas took place: so that, in process of time, people who understood one another heretofore, could not converse; hence misunderstandings, misrepresentations, enmities, evil-speaking, war, &c. *On.*

Nimrod arose and opposed himself to Peleg. Now Nimrod was a man whose way of life was opponent to inclosures, for he was a hunter; he ranged the lands, and slew the beasts of the field, with an arrow from the bow. He spake against the sayings of Peleg; but it came to pass, that Peleg was mightier than Nimrod. Wherefore Nimrod said unto those that were with him: Let us also build us cities to dwell in, lest Peleg and those that are with him be too many for us. This was the beginning of the kingdom of Babylon, and Nimrod was the first king thereof. *Phinehas.*

Notes on Chap. III.

NOW had the world subsisted about two thousand years, and from their dispersion and different views and interests, different modes of worship had arisen; men had forsaken the precepts of the patriarchs, the natural worship of the Deity; set up symbols of the Deity; worshipped in groves, estranged themselves concerning the truth; their ideas became, through vice, circumscribed; the discerning few now got rule; irregularity and punishment stalked. Abraham, seeing the defection of his brethren, counselled them to return to the ways of old; but they had gone so far astray, and had so bewildered themselves, that they could not return to their primitive way of worship and life. This obliged Abraham to leave their society, that he, and his family, might serve the Lord, persuaded, that if he, and his, walked uprightly, that from him would arise a great people, by whose example the nations would be led to serve the Lord. *Hur.*

Tradition saith, That the patriarch Abraham heard a voice as from heaven, commanding him to slay his son Isaac, as he was in the field alone by himself. Abraham returns to his wife Sarah disconsolate. Sarah enquires the cause, and Abraham tells her, that a voice from heaven had said unto him, Take thy son, and slay him, and offer him up a burnt-offering in the land wherein he was born. Upon this, Sarah, who was a woman of great wisdom and discernment, expostulated with Abraham, and convinced him that it could not be the voice of God; and her argument was very conclusive: If the holy voice has said, Of thee I will make a great nation, the holy voice cannot say *this*, because if thou slayest thy son, how can the former be fulfilled? *Hur.*

Notes on Chap. IV.

JASHER takes no notice why Joseph was advanced in the court of Pharaoh; and therefore it may be presumed, that so many stories were extant, that he could not with certainty adopt one. However, the most probable I will here set down, as a remark on that part of Jasher which concerns Joseph. Joseph was the beloved of Jacob, and obtained leave of his father, to travel into Egypt; for, says he, there will be a famine in the land of Canaan, and I will go and provide corn for you and my brethren at Zoan, that ye perish not. Accordingly, Joseph had not been long at Zoan before there happened to be a great increase of corn in that land; but in the land of Canaan, the earth brought not forth. Now Pharaoh sent and gathered together all the wise men of his kingdom, and he said unto them: Behold, the earth giveth of its increase, thrice told, and there is as much more food for the people than they want, and moreover the hands are not equal to the harvest! what shall we do? And the wise men knew not. And it was proclaimed, saying, Whosoever shall resolve the thing, he shall stand before Pharaoh. And it was told unto Pharaoh, that Joseph, the stranger, the son of Jacob, who dwelt at Hebron, in the land of Canaan, could unfold the secret. Then Pharaoh called for Joseph, and Pharaoh said unto him, Speak. Then Joseph bowed himself before Pharaoh, and said, The Lord God of his fathers had revealed it unto him, that there should be great plenty in Egypt, and that there would be great dearth in the land of Canaan, which dearth was then actually begun; wherefore, O king, build storehouses in every city, and buy ye of the Egyptians the surplus of their abundance; peradventure this time of plenty will be succeeded by a time of want and scarcity. Then Pharaoh advanced Joseph. *Phinehas.*

There is but one expression in Jasher which points at all the evils which the administration of Joseph brought on the Egyptians, it is this; And he was a stranger in the land of Egypt: and he bought Egypt with a price. The Egyptians, before the advancement of Joseph, was a free people; they paid no tax towards the support of the government, nor of the priesthood. As Joseph had prophesied, so it came to pass: the time of plenty was succeeded by a time of want and scarcity. And then it was, that he sold unto the people at a great price, the increase he had before bought for a very low price. When he had exhausted the money, and the jewels of the people, and brought the wealth of Egypt into the king's coffers, and the people still wanted food, he then bargains with them that they should pawn their lands. And when the dearth was over, then it came to pass, that all Egypt by a perpetual decree rendered the fifth of its increase unto Pharaoh. *Phinehas.*

The Hebrews were oppressed by the Egyptians by a taxation, and which was as a brick for hardness. When Pharaoh saw that they were become a great people for number, he sent unto them, that they should bear some part of the public burthen, towards the maintenance and dignity of the state; he alledged, that when the famine was in the land of Canaan, the corn of Egypt saved their lives; and therefore they should give them the tenth of their increase, of their flocks, of their herds, and of their grounds. The children of Israel, who had lived free from the least demand of any kind, for three hundred years and upwards, regarded this imposition, as a brick, that is, as a hard thing, and were uneasy under it. *Hur.*

Notes on Chap. V.

MIRIAM was born fifteen years before Moses. She was the daughter of Amram, by Jochebed, his wife; one who to great natural parts added that of great thought and foresight. The decree coming forth, that the Hebrew males should all be slain as they were born, and she having heard how good-natured the daughter of Pharaoh was, proposed to her parents, that she would carry her brother Moses, and meet the princess as she walked by the river side, which was the custom of the princess every morning to do, and seem as though she was going to drown the infant. By which means, says Miriam, when the princess beholdeth the child, peradventure she may enquire what I am about to do with the infant. Then will I answer, and say, I am going to drown it, it being an infant male of the children of Jacob, according to the decree of Pharaoh, thy father, which says, Every male that openeth the womb, among the children of Jacob, shall ye drown in the river. O, says Jochebed, thou art as a sea of bitterness unto me! O my daughter, thou hast ingulphed me in an ocean of perplexity! Be not afraid, says Miriam, whether is it not all one, that he perish by the hands and command of the daughter of Pharaoh, or by the slayers of infants; we cannot always hide him from knowledge. The morn arose, the sun rejoiced to run his course, and all nature smiled, when Miriam, almost by force, takes up the lovely infant, whose innocent looks were enough to engage every eye, and away she carries him to the banks of the river, to meet the princess. Jochebed and Amram follow at some distance, waiting the event. The princess was taking her morning walk, attended by her women. Now Miriam had placed herself under a tree, where she knew the princess would pass by, and was there kissing, and taking, as it were, her last farewell of her brother, and as the princess approached, was swaddling it up, that with the greater convenience she might throw it into the river, and then she kisses it again, and the tears flowed from her eyes. The princess and the ladies stood at some distance, viewing and thinking what the meaning of this thing could be; and seeing that the young woman looked at the water, and then at the child, imagined that she was going to drown it. Upon this, the princess calls earnestly to Miriam, and asks her, what she was going to do with the infant? Miriam advances, and says, I am about to drown it, even as Pharaoh has commanded. How! says the princess, sure Pharaoh has not said it. Then answered Miriam, Thy father hath said, Every male that openeth the womb, among the children of Jacob, shall ye drown in the river. And this is the first which hath opened the womb since the decree hath been made. And the princess said, Give me the child. Miriam having delivered the child, the princess enquires for one to nurse it. Here Miriam produces his mother, Jochebed, to be a nurse for her brother. And the princess said, He shall be my son, and his name shall be called Moses, because I have taken him from the water, wherein he was to be drowned. Then Jochebed took Moses, and returned unto her house, and she said to her daughter, Behold, now thou art unto me as an uplifting. Aaron, at this time, was three years old. The princess that very day went unto Pharaoh, and got the decree revoked. Thus did Miriam, when fifteen years of age, contrive the revoking of the decree of Pharaoh, concerning the murder of the infant males of the children of Israel.

Hur, out of the book of Aaron.

Miriam from hence became the admired of the Hebrews: every tongue sang of her praise. She taught Israel; she tutored the children of Jacob; and the people called her, by way of eminence, The Teacher. She studied the good of the nation, and Aaron and the people hearkened unto her. To her the people bowed; to her the afflicted came. Israel enjoyed peace all the time of the days of the princess, who succoured Moses. Miriam was ninety-five years of age, when Moses came from Midian. And Aaron was eighty and three. And Moses was eighty years of age. *Hur, out of the Book of Aaron.*

It was a tradition in my time, that the princess carried Moses to her father, and by shewing him the infant, and expostulating with him concerning the barbarity of those who had counselled the decree, prevailed on the king to revoke it. *Hur.*

Notes on Chap. VI.

MOSES, who till now, had lived altogether in the court of Pharaoh, leaves Zoan, and goes into Goshen to visit his brethren, the Hebrews: when there, he encourages them to revolt from the Egyptians. Pharaoh hearing of this, Moses thought it best to fly into Midian, being then forty years of age. There he marries Zipporah, the daughter of Jethro, who was the son of Esau, who was the son of Isaac. Jethro was a great man; one who had given laws to his people, and was both a king and a priest. He was a worshipper of the true God, but did not use circumcision among his people; yet he ordained a priesthood, and appointed the observation of sabbaths, and of feasts, and kept holy days. There was a particular enmity notwithstanding, betwixt the descendants of Jacob and those of Esau; and Jacob had particularly cautioned his children not to marry among the uncircumcised. Jethro, finding that Moses was a man of great policy, and versed in all the learning and magic of the Egyptians, gives him his eldest daughter, Zipporah, to wife; by whom Moses had two sons, Gershom and Eliezar. At the expiration of forty years afterwards, Moses is told by Jethro, that Pharaoh, who sought his life, was dead; is advised to go up into Egypt, to endeavour to bring his brethren from under the yoke of Pharaoh into the wilderness, and there to make them a separate people, under a particular government of their own. Moses, flushed with the thoughts of success, brings out of Midian, Zipporah and her two sons, and comes into Goshen: but the elders knew him not, and tell him, that he had transgressed the precepts of Jacob, in marrying Zipporah. Upon which disgust of the Hebrews, Moses sends Zipporah, and her two sons, back to Jethro. *Hur.*

And it came to pass, during the time Moses was in Midian, which was the space of forty years, that Caleb, who was a ruler among the sons of Jacob, and a mighty man, invented the arrow, and the bow, and trained up the males to the use of it, and he, and his followers, became expert in it. This was a contrivance that was more excellent than the javelin: he found he could kill the enemy hereby at a great distance; wherefore the Hebrews in this respect became too mighty for the Egyptians. *Othniel.*

Notes on Chap. VII. VIII. IX. X. XI.

MOSES persuades the Hebrews to leave Goshen, and go into the wilderness. They ask of him a sign: he gives them many, which they believe. But Pharaoh, when Moses went to him, would not believe. After many persuasions, with the advice of all his princes, Pharaoh lets them go upon certain conditions, which the Epyptians told him the Hebrews had not performed; at which Pharaoh was provoked, and pursues Moses and the people. Of which Moses having intelligence, he changes his course, and (when at the extremity of the Red Sea, purposing to lead the Hebrews to the foot of mount Sinai. and put them under the protection of the Midianites, lest Pharaoh should pursue him, and in his rage slay the Hebrews,) turns off towards Baal-zephon, in which neighbourhood Moses encamped. When Pharaoh and his host came to Etham, seven days after Moses had left the place, he was informed, that Moses, instead of going straight forward into the wilderness, was gone to Baal-zephon. Here Pharaoh stops, his troops being fatigued with a sudden and hasty march, and sends to demand of Moses satisfaction for what injury the Hebrews had done the Egyptians. Upon this, Moses sends Jasher to tell Pharaoh, that he would search out the offenders, and deliver them up, and such restitution should be made as should be satisfactory to them, and that this should be done by the fourth day. To this Pharaoh agreed, indeed he was necessitated to stay, for his troops were so harassed and faint, that they wanted rest. Moses, having thus gained time, disposes the march of his people over the sands of the Red Sea, in the manner following: He ordered Aaron to lead the van into the sea, at the recess of the water; they went in, a man and a woman; the women carrying and leading the infants, and the men carrying the baggage. Thus did they march; the tribe of Levi and the tribe of Joseph got over that reflux; the next, the tribe of Judah and the tribe of Simeon; the next, the tribe of Benjamin and the tribe of Ephraim; the next, the tribe of Zebulun and the tribe of Issachar; the next, the tribe of Dan and the half-tribe of Manasseh; the next, the half-tribe of Manasseh, and all the women and children of the tribe of Reuben and the tribe of Gad, with their baggage. Moses having thus dismissed all, except the men of Reuben and Gad, about midnight blew the trumpet, and he led the people through the sea with a hasty march, for which he had prepared them by sending away their wives, children, and baggage. Moses had so well contrived to cut off all intercourse between the Hebrews and the Egyptians, that the latter knew not that the former had fled. On the fourth day, in the morning, Pharaoh sends to demand restitution, but behold Moses with the tribes of Reuben and Gad had crossed the Red Sea, in the preceding night. They hastened unto Pharaoh, and told him, that the Hebrews fled by the way of the Red Sea; (for there was a road which led through there, at the reflux, for foot-passengers, but was not at all commodious for horses and chariots.) Now during the time that Moses and the tribes passed through the sea, by night the moon shone; but afterwards, the dark nights came on and the rains fell. Pharaoh pursued Moses to Baal-zephon, and there he was told in what manner the Hebrews passed the sands of the Red Sea. At this, Pharaoh was greatly disheartened, and he said, Let us return from whence we came, for we cannot go over the sands with our horses and chariots; and could we cross with part of the host of Egypt, for all cannot pass at one reflux, the Hebrews will slay us. Wherefore Pharaoh cursed the people of Jacob, he and all the host of Egypt, and returned to Zoan. *Hur.*

Every one knows the famous miracle of the passage over the Red Sea, when the Lord opened this sea, dried it up, and made the Israelites pass through it, dry-shod, to the number of 600,000, without reckoning old men, women, or children. Some ancient authors have advanced, that Moses, having lived long near the Red Sea, in the country of Midian, had observed that it kept its regular ebbing and flowing, like the ocean; so that taking the advantage of the time of the ebb, he led the Hebrews over; but the Egyptians, not knowing the nature of the sea, and rashly entering into it just before the return of the tide, were all swallowed up, and drowned, as Moses relates. Thus the priests of Memphis explained it; and this opinion has been adopted by a great number of moderns.

In the queries of Michaelis sent to Niebuhr, when in Egypt, it was proposed to him to enquire upon the spot, "Whether there were not some ridges of rocks where the water was shallow, so that an army at particular times may pass over?" Secondly, "Whether the Etesian winds, which blow strongly all the summer from the North West, could not blow so violently against the sea, as to keep it back on a heap, so that the Israelites might have passed without a miracle?"

A copy of these queries was left also for Mr. Bruce, the traveller, who justly observed as follows: "I must confess, however learned the gentlemen were who proposed these doubts, I did not think they merited any attention to solve them."

This passage is told us by Scripture to be a miraculous one; and, if so, we have nothing to do with natural causes.

If we do not believe Moses, we need not believe the transaction at all, seeing that it is from his authority alone we derive it. If we believe in God, that he made the sea, we must believe he can divide it when he sees a proper reason; and of that he must be the only judge. It is no greater miracle to divide the Red Sea, than to divide the river Jordan.

If the Eastern wind, blowing from the North West in summer, could keep up the sea, as a wall on the right, or to the South, of fifty feet high, still the difficulty would remain of building the wall on the left hand, or to the North; besides, water standing in that position for a day, must have lost the nature of fluid.

Whence came that cohesion of particles which hindered that wall to escape at the sides? This is as great a miracle as that of Moses. If the Etesian winds had done this once, they must have repeated it many a time before and since, from the same causes. It appears however, from the accurate observations of Niebuhr and Bruce, that there is no ledge of rocks running across the gulph anywhere, to afford a shallow passage.

The second query, about the Etesian, or Northerly wind, is refuted by the express mention of a strong Easterly wind blowing across, and scooping out a dry passage; not that it was necessary for Omnipotence to employ it there as an instrument, any more than at Jordan; but it seems to be introduced in the sacred history by way of anticipation, to exclude the natural agency that might in after times be employed for solving the miracle. It is remarkable, that the monsoon in the Red Sea blows the summer half of the year from the North, the winter half, from the South; neither of which would produce the miracle in question.

The tides in this sea are moderate. At Suez the difference between high and low waters did not exceed from three to four feet, according to Niebuhr's observations on the tides in that gulph, during the years 1762, and 1763. It is evident from the text of Moses, and other sacred authors, who have mentioned this miraculous passage, that no other account is supportable, than that which supposes the Hebrews to cross over the sea from shore to shore, in a vast space of dry ground, which was left void by the waters at their retiring. (Exod. xiv. 16, 17, &c.)

In the canticle that Moses sang at their coming out of the Red Sea, he says (Exod. xv. 8.) "With the blast of thy nostrils (or, with the wind of thy fury,) the waters were gathered together; the flood stood upright as an heap; and the depths were congealed in the heart of the sea." The Psalmist says (Psalm, lxxviii. 13.) "He divided the sea, and caused them to pass through, and he made the waters to stand as on a heap." He says in another place, "That the sea fled at the sight of God." (Psalm, cxiv. 3, 5.) "That the Lord made himself a path in the sea, that He walked in the midst of the waters." (Psalm, lxxvii. 19.) Isaiah, lxiii. 11, &c. says, "That the Lord divided the waves before his people; that He conducted them through the bottom of the abyss, as a horse is led through the midst of a field." Habbakuk, iii. 15, says, "That the Lord made himself a road to drive his chariot and horses across the sea, across the mud of great waters." Lastly, the author of the book of Wisdom, xix. 7, 8, 10, 17, 18, says, "That the dry land appeared all on a sudden in a place where water was before; that a free passage was opened in a moment through the midst of the Red Sea; and that a green field was seen in the midst of the abyss, &c.:" It is thought the place where the Hebrews passed by the Red Sea, is two or three leagues below its Northern point, at the place called Kolsum, or Clysma.

Dr. Hales observes, that "It sufficiently appears, even from Niebuhr's own statement, that the passage of the Israelites could not have taken place near Suez: For, first, he evidently confounded the town of Kolsum, the ruins of which he places near Suez, and where he supposed the passage to be made, with the Bay of Kolsum, which began about forty-five miles lower down, as Bryant has satisfactorily proved, from the astronomical observations of Ptolemy and Ulug Beigh, made at Heroum, the ancient head of the gulph. 2ndly, Instead of crossing the sea at or near Etham, their second station, the Israelites "turned southwards, along the western shore; and their third station at Pihahiroth or Bedea, was at least a full day's journey below Etham; as Bryant has satisfactorily proved from Scripture. (Exod. xiv. 2.) Hales' New Analysis of Chronology, vol. i. page 388, to 391.: Wells's Geography of the Old and New Testament, vol. i. page 240. *Editor.*

It was at this time, and on the account of the fraud Moses and his people had put on the Egyptians, that they were called יעקבי or יעקבים that is, Jacobites. *Ehud.*

Miriam first stepped into the Red Sea, amidst the thousands of Israel, who thereupon cried out, Behold the queen of the sea. When all her people were safe in the wilderness, she proclaimed a feast, at which Miriam and the women of Israel leaped for joy. *Hur.*

The people of Israel, soon after they had left the borders of the Red Sea, and had journeyed for three days into the wilderness, had exhausted their water, and thereupon was in great distress, and they said, Where shall we now have water to drink? Moses, in this emergency, assembles the elders. Miriam was one of the assembly, for she being the admired of the people, they proceeded to no business till she was present; nay, so deep was her penetration, and so exquisite her judgment, that her word was final. She advised that they should dig for water. *Hur.*

The great wisdom and policy of Moses is here very conspicuous, in his selling to the Egyptians, for their gold and silver, all the possessions of the Hebrews. By this means, they had wherewithal, when they had gotten into the wilderness, to purchase oxen, sheep, and all the necessaries of life, of the Amalekites, the Hivites, &c. and also all utensils of husbandry, and horses, &c. for their immediate use. *Othniel.*

The riches the Hebrews carried with them procured them the friendship, at least, the indulgence, of the people of the nations, for the trade of gold for the fruits of their land made them rich. This Miriam perceived would in time impoverish her own people, wherefore she advised them to till the ground, and to tame the beasts of the field. *Jazer.*

It seemeth plain, that the Egyptians intended to buy the possessions of the Hebrews for a very small sum, and thereby to oppress them grievously: but this scheme of Moses and the elders to sell more in number of every thing than they had, outwitted them, and flung their iniquity upon their own heads. Besides, Moses by this means brought his own people the more readily into his designs of shaking off the power of Egypt. *Zadock.*

Miriam might justly be stiled, the mother of the Hebrew nation, in a proper sense, for she taught them first to dig for water. She likewise stimulated them to till the ground, and cultivate the tree. She brought a grain out of Egypt, and sowed the field. The male and female of the flock and herd did she bring. *Tobias.*

Notes on Chap. XV.

THE contest between Moses and Miriam was concerning the establishment of the laws and customs prescribed by Jethro. She argued and reasoned very wisely. Are not the laws and customs of the children of Jacob sufficient to govern the people, seeing they have done so for four hundred years? Surely the wisdom of our forefathers is greater than that of the Midianites. The people took the side of Miriam. *Hur.*

Miriam opposed the introduction of the laws given by Jethro. She well knew, that if Zipporah was suffered to dwell among the children of Israel, of consequence, the customs of Midian would take place, that intermarriages would happen, and that such practices would tend to the ingulphing them in the nations. *Jezer.*

All the days of the life of Miriam were one hundred and twenty years. In her time the Israelites received no other laws and customs, save those from Abraham, Isaac, and Jacob. The patriarchs in every family ruled. *Jazer.*

When the people of the nations, the Moabites, the Perrizzites, the Hivites, the Amorites, the Jebusites, and the Hittites, heard that Miriam was dead, they were moved; and the reason was, because she restrained Moses from destroying them. *Othniel.*

Notes on Chap XVI. XVII. XVIII.

MOSES, soon after the death of Miriam, orders Nadab and Abihu to build an altar nigh unto mount Sinai, and to raise twelve tables or pillars for each tribe to come unto. When this was done, he appoints twelve young men, of great strength, to slay oxen, and sheep, and lambs, and roast them on the altar: and Moses blew the trumpet, and he proclaimed a feast, and every tribe assembled each to his pillar or station, and they sat down, and they did eat. And this was the first public feast of the Israelites. And now it was, that they chose out seventy elders for to be with Moses, and to judge the people. *Hur.*

Moses, after the contest with Miriam, never attempted to establish the laws of Jethro till some time after her death. He had a design to secrete her, imagining, if it had not been for her humane disposition, he should have been able to have settled the people in Canaan during his life, which would have been for the good of the commonweal: but the policy of Moses was for killing and destroying all before him: the policy of Miriam was the reverse. Miriam dying, they remained for a short time in the method she left them; but as the people could not now apply unto her for wisdom, they were at a great loss, and that loss grew daily more and more perceptible.

At length, the complaints reached the ear of Moses. In order to redress the grievance, Moses advises the people to elect such persons as they should think capable of judging the people. That the people should elect, was pleasing to the multitude; by which means Moses had seventy to assist him in the administration. The first thing Moses proposed, and which they agreed to, was the admission and adoption of Zipporah and her sons. Moses soon after assumed the title of king; and having brought Nadab and Abihu, and the seventy elders who spake for the people, into his plan of forming the Hebrew monarchy, they assembled on mount Sinai, and, together with Jethro, fixed on the rule of government. *Phinehas.*

In the following chapters nothing occurs, but what fully accords with the statements of Moses, the Jewish Lawgiver, only with relation to Miriam, who seems from the statements of Jasher, to have held a very high place in the councils of the elders of Israel, so that no important step was taken without her concurrence. In one instance, she appears to have resisted Moses, on which account she was struck with leprosy, but again restored at his successful prayer: and although she resisted the adoption of Zipporah into the commonwealth of Israel, she did it from a conscientious motive, dread'ng the influence of the Midianitish women, and th pollution of the Jews by intermarriages with them, which soon was the case.

The laws and customs proposed by Jethro, she also rejected, arguing, that the statutes and ordinances of Jacob were preferable to them, and that as they had hitherto prospered under the ancient government, by the fathers and heads of the tribes, there could be no sufficient cause for their departure from them. However, at length, the whole of the ceremonial law took effect; Moses by miracles and signs, and mighty wonders, proving that he acted by divine authority, so that all opposition ceased, and the government was fully established in a Sanhedrim of seventy elders, Moses being king in Jeshurun.

It appea s that Jasher was eminent in his days, not only for the integrity, but for the prosperity of his government; that his conduct, in every relation and capacity, was unexceptionable; and that he died in a good ol l age, full of honour, and much lamented by the nation, being one hundred and twelve years old. The book written by him, was kept with religious veneration, and though not of equal authority with the books of Moses, yet was appealed to both in the times of Joshua, and the great king of Israel, David

Thus, then, it appears, that as far as such a work can be authenticated, this possesses every proof of being a transcript of the original manuscript: and, consequently, that it is worthy to be preserved as a collateral evidence of the facts detailed more fully in the writings of Moses, the book of Joshua, and the book of Judges. Let us therefore make a due improvement hereof, by imitating the uprightness of Jasher, obeying the precepts delivered by him, and yielding an unreserved obedience to that better covenant under which we live, knowing that the whole economy of the Jews, adumbrated and typified the better covenant of grace, in the person of our glorious Redeemer, who hath obtained for us a better inheritance than Canaan, even an inheritance incorruptible, undefiled, and that fadeth not away, reserved in heaven for us.

Editor.

ROSE, PRINTER, BROADMEAD, BRISTOL.